BLACK AND WHITE LIKE YOU & ME

Parallel Lines Sometimes Intersect

THOMAS F. DANIELS & THOMAS C. MARSH

Cover design by Tremble Creative Services | tremblecreative.com
Cover image | Detroit News | Downtown Detroit 1963
Copy editing by Nikki Massie, MA | pouchparty@gmail.com

ORDERING INFORMATION:

Quantity sales. Special discounts are available on quantity purchases by corporations, associations and others. Book signings and appearances can be arranged with the publisher at TomJoMedia@gmail.com.

www.BlackandWhiteLikeYouandMe.com

Printed in the United States of America.

Black and White Like You and Me.

ISBN: 978-1-946653-00-0

DEDICATION

Joan Daniels & Annette Marsh

What would we be without them? We are happy that we never found out. Of course, we are talking about our wives Joan Daniels and Annette Marsh. Thank you for being there as we developed into good husbands, fathers, and grandfathers. We never would have without you.

Although this book is not about marital relationships, it has caused us to stop and reflect on the past of which you were so much a part. We have told you so many times about our upbringing that we are sure that you think you were actually there. In Cookie's case, Annette actually was there for most of it having met her in junior high.

Thank you for being a patient listener. Thank you for supporting this project. Thank you for being you.

BLACK AND WHITE LIKE YOU & ME

Parallel Lines
Sometimes Intersect

To Amber,

Tom Daniel

Tom "Cookie" Marsh Sr

Thanks
2019

FOREWORD

There was a rumbling coming from sections of the city going mostly unnoticed.

Even though Detroit was experiencing prosperity and unprecedented population growth in the 1940s, citizens soon would have to confront the reality that they could no longer live in their safe "parallel universe." For those of our generation, it appeared that the volcano would continue to growl until it erupted into the ultimate explosion: "The Civil Disobedience of 1967." There had been all the prophecy needed in the Detroit's Race Riot of 1943 and the Kercheval Riot of 1966 to understand that things were not right with the town and its leadership.

But I have gotten ahead of myself. To a child born in the late 1940s or early 1950s, separate but equal – or, should we say unequal - didn't mean just schooling but daily life as well. Black and white children born at this time entered a world where they would live parallel lives, but as youngsters, they didn't realize it.

To us, all was normal. We played and socialized mostly with those of our own race. Our views, right or wrong, of "other people" were formed by views passed down by parents, family, friends, politicians, and established institutions.

When Cookie's father migrated to Detroit, he had two choices of where to move his family – either the west side, which was bounded by Tireman, Grand River, Buchanan, and Central Streets or "The Black Bottom." This area of the lower east side was not named for the color of its residents but for the farming soil the French settlers found upon discovering Detroit.

This district was mostly located south of Gratiot Avenue running from Jefferson on the south to an area called Paradise Valley on the north end. These two black districts were "renewed" in the late 50s and early 60s by demolition and expressways. The black population was displaced. Hastings was the spine of the Black Bottom neighborhood with black businesses not only created on Hastings but also spinning out on streets like Beaubien, Adams, Mack, St. Antoine, Forest, and others.

Subsequently, most white residents of Detroit thought this area was unsafe, filled with drugs, prostitution, and seedy night clubs. This isolation and segregation, however, allowed blacks to bond together.

Out of necessity, the African-Americans became entrepreneurs creating businesses to serve the black community. Grocery stores, restaurants, bars, funeral homes, and newspapers were all black owned and operated. Owning their own businesses was a godsend since most blacks did menial jobs: garbage collection, domestics, and the dirty, lower paying jobs in the factories.

During this time and unbeknownst to most whites, there was a strong group of emerging professionals. Through the training ground of black churches, social clubs such as cotillion clubs, black schools and colleges, the community began to produce highly trained professionals: doctors, dentists, teachers, and lawyers.

This legion of professionals used their knowledge of civil rights law. Names like Damon Keith, John Conyers, and George Crockett became heroes in the eyes of black Detroiters and would impact southeastern Michigan and the nation in the years to come.

This was the world that the children of the late 1940s and early 1950s entered. By the time these same children reached their teen years, there would be an inevitable collision. The parallel lives that they had been experiencing would now intersect.

Bob "Spider" Daniels

PURPOSE

The most segregated day of the week is Sunday followed by Saturday when people congregate at their individual, isolated places of worship. I wonder what God thinks when he looks down on the Sabbath Day only to see his children cloister themselves in divisive settings. It is no wonder that there is so much discrimination and hatred in the world. It is crazy to think that on what should be the holiest day(s) of the week that we have nothing to do with each other. I would be just as surprised to see African-Americans in a Catholic church as I would if I saw them at a Jewish synagogue.

I am sure that African-Americans would be equally surprised to see me at their Baptist and African Methodist Church. Perhaps Sunday mornings would be better served meeting and socializing with members of the other race? We know as parents that we are only as happy as our most unhappy child. God the Father is asking, "Can't we all just get along?"

Speaking of getting along and crossing parallel lines, my daughter Jessy and I attended an Easter production called *Perilous Times* down at the Masonic Auditorium produced by another African-American friend and geezer Ty Hemphill. Milt Andrew, a former Detroit Public Schools elementary school principal, met us there to view the production. Milt is African-American as well and a great role model.

In fact, on this evening he brought along another man by the name of Thomas. Thomas was crippled and never could have attended if Milt hadn't literally carried Thomas up those steep auditorium steps. 99% of the full house audience was African-American. Why? It was a great musical depicting the final days of Jesus Christ. Should that have been attended by blacks only?

We are hopeful that this book will begin to open the eyes and hearts of whites and blacks and that by enjoying these anecdotes about two people, the readers will realize that the answer to fear, prejudice, and hatred is to meet, converse, and interact with the other race.

We also hope that by reading this book, the readers will reminisce about their own lives and realize that they are no different than Cookie and I. We hope that readers will find their common bond, as Cookie and I have with basketball, causing them to cross their parallel lines.

Thomas F. Daniels

CHAPTER 1

Introductions

Thomas Curtis Marsh | black

I was born September 24, 1951 in Laurel, Mississippi, lived in Detroit, Michigan my whole life except for summer visits down south. My parents sent me to public school and brought me up in church. I have an older brother John and two older twin sisters Clarice and Clorice.

When I was little I loved cookies and would charm my Great Aunt into making them for me. She began to call me her "cookie nephew." The nickname has stuck all these years, except now people just call me Cookie. If you are in the city of Detroit and you mention Cookie Marsh, most people will know who I am.

I graduated with a degree in social work from the University of Detroit and married my wife Annette on December 10, 1983. I have seven children: Lawanda, Lalisa, Lamont, Candis, Jemiel, Javon, and Thomas III.

Fatherhood and basketball have been extremely important in my life. I am so proud of the fact that all of my children get along, have a relationship with each other, and are there to help each other when needed. We all get together for barbecues and holidays and some of us even go on vacations together to our annual trip to Cancun, Jamaica or other Caribbean resorts.

My ancestors can be traced to slavery and African roots. I realize the fear, anger, and hardship these relatives went through only for one reason: the color of their skin which they had no control over. I remember the story my father told about when he was in the military in Asia somewhere. Thinking that they were funny, some white soldiers told the Asians that black people had tails. My father said that the Asians would always be walking behind him trying to get a glimpse of his tail. My father told that story with a laugh, but deep down it had to hurt him being compared to some animal. My mother and father settled into Mississippi because that is where their parents and grandparents were born. Obviously, they had no control of how they looked or where they lived during their younger years.

My dear, deceased father, in search of a better life for himself and his family, heard of work at the car companies in Detroit, Michigan in the early 1950s.

Just as a side note, Henry Ford can be credited for the black exodus from the South. In 1900, there were barely 5,000 blacks in the City of Detroit. Henry Ford, who had been an equal opportunity employer long before those words became the catch phrase and law of today, hired a William Perry and the city of Detroit became an attraction for southern blacks in search of the promised five dollars per day salary which was paid equally to all workers.

Getting back to my father, can you imagine the courage it took for him to uproot leaving everything familiar behind? Can you perceive the fear he must have faced in order to find a better opportunity for him and subsequently for me? I adore him for that decision. Coming to Detroit afforded him a job, a better way to make a living.

But where would he live? The choices for blacks were limited to say the very least. Spider wrote in the Foreword about the Black Bottom area. My father settled us in at the Jeffries Project which I will discuss later on. He left the comfortable and familiar surroundings of relatives and environment and cast himself into a place of chaos and confusion. The Temptations song "Ball of Confusion" would have been perfect for him only it was created many years later.

Despite enduring so many racial slights, my father told me:

> "The only way you would ever look down on another person
> is if you were reaching to help him up."

He would point out the Bible passages: "Don't judge, lest ye be judged" and "Love thy neighbor as thyself." I can honestly say that those teachings have affected my way of thinking my entire life.

Again, I thank my father for showing me how to cope with a difficult world.

Thomas Frank Daniels | white

I was born September 30, 1948, in Detroit, Michigan. My parents Frank and Rebecca raised my older brother Bob and my younger sister Mary and, of course, me. I lived in Michigan my whole life except for a short two year stint in Rapid City, South Dakota during 1980-82.

I had a Catholic school upbringing, sixteen years including college at University of Detroit with a major in English and a teaching degree. In 1983, I married my wife Joan who had two children Jared and Nick. I contributed four children to the equation from a former marriage: Jacob, Jessica, Joshua, and Jenna.

My nickname is "Whitey." Now before you make a snap judgment about that name, it has nothing to do with race. Originally it had to do with the *Bowery Boys*, 1940s movies and eventually television series similar to the *Three Stooges* but about tough kids and their antics. My brother Bob was nicknamed "Satch," a Bowery boy. "Whitey" was another Bowery boy.

As the name continued to follow me, it evolved into the color of my skin. I am two shades darker than an albino! As a matter of fact, I have always wanted one or more of my children to marry and have children with a tall African-American before the Daniels' clan turned into albino pygmies. We are relatively short as well.

My ancestry can be traced to German/Polish on my father's side and British on my mother's side. My maternal grandmother was a member of the D.A.R. (Daughters of the American Revolution). It seems that people are curious as to "how did they get here." *Roots* was a popular television series as well as that PBS show called *Who Do You Think You Are?* that traces celebrities' family trees. Ancestry.com is a mammoth website as well. My mother left North Carolina following her sister, my Aunt Margaret, to Detroit in the early 1940s. She met my father, and here I am.

No one has ever had control over to whom he or she was born. If we did, what choices would we have made? Would we want to be born in the same socioeconomic condition? Would we want the same mother, father, and relatives? Would we want to live in the same state or even the same country? Would we have wanted to be black or white? For those of us who believe, this birth was in God's plan. Heck, my mother always said that my propensity to having a protruding stomach was due to the Heath side of her family. No sit-ups could ever conquer that condition. I personally always thought it was due to the amount of beer I used to drink!

But anyway, the point is why do we put so much emphasis on what people look like? They had no choice in the matter. It always troubled me that kids would be teased even to the point of bullying because of what they looked like.

As former Dean of Students at Brother Rice High School, I would emphatically explain to the perpetrators the error of their thinking and acting.

I worked for over thirty years in an affluent high school where most students had everything they needed and wanted. One student drove a Maserati to school. Another was often late because his valet service was slow in bringing his car up to the house in the morning. As with Cookie, I grew up getting most of what I needed and very little of what I wanted.

My point is this: so effing what? Those were the cards that we were dealt. Life is learning how to make the best of the blessings we were given and to use the opportunities that presented themselves.

Unfortunately, because of the cards that Cookie and I were dealt, our parallel lines did not cross until we were in our middle age. Certainly, the color of our skin was a contributing factor to never having met.

CHAPTER 2

Geezerball

Thomas "Cookie" Marsh | *black*

Geezerball is made up of guys mostly over the age of fifty. We still enjoy playing the game of basketball. We have some younger guys mixed in with us. These guys are in their late twenties to early thirties and into the early forties. These are relatives or related to other guys by employment or school.

GEEZERBALL TEAM

But the thing about Geezerball is that it is more than just a game. We play the game of basketball, and it is very intense. However, we don't have the same problems as when I play with guys of my own race when the game could possibly end up with a guy maybe even be threatened to be shot. If you made the wrong move or you didn't like what somebody did on the court, I would hear someone threaten to do bodily harm – not often, but once is enough.

At age sixty, what are we going to do to hurt someone? Snatch our canes and beat each other across the head with our walking sticks? Not hardly. The thing about Geezerball is that it is the same game of basketball but without all the arguing and cheating and without the great egos. I know we all have egos, but we put them aside and just try to play the game the way it was meant to be played: play hard but fair.

Geezerball is a privilege. We had guys who had to stop coming to the gym because they argued too much, fussing, and ending up in some kind of negative commotion.

The group culminated in us going to a forty-five and over tournament in Toronto. We went there for the very first time and won the championship. Now I know that because it was in amateur or recreation ball that this was no big deal, but for us, man, that was like winning the NBA championship. This was our very first time in the tournament, black and white guys playing on the same team and winning and beating teams that had won in that tournament for years. We were able to pull it off because we assembled one of the best teams that I ever played on, and not to be bragging, yes, I am a high school ex-All American, played college basketball for the University of Detroit, was the captain of the team, was the all-time leading scorer for Detroit Northern. If you don't believe me, check the record books. Don't walk around with your nose all snotty; if you don't know, you better ask somebody.

Geezerball is a thing that I have grown to really love, and I pray that I will be able to enjoy it well past the age of sixty-five. I thank all the guys who have been involved black, white, Hispanic. I especially thank Ron Teasley who invited me to play that very first time at Brother Rice High School. It is just a joy. We look forward to it, and it has brought us closer together. As it says in philosophy, shared experiences bring people closer together. This shared experience of Geezerball has certainly brought all of us closer together in terms of us and our families knowing each other and being supportive of one another. I thank Tom Daniels for allowing me to be a part of Geezerball.

TORONTO CHAMPIONSHIP

Thomas "Whitey" Daniels | *white*

To say that Gene Seaborn broke the color barrier for Geezerball is really not accurate. True, Gene is African-American and a terrific basketball player and, relatively speaking, a geezer. However, back in 1985 when we began playing half-court pickup basketball at Covington Middle School in Bloomfield Hills, Michigan, Gene was a pioneer, an original. In fact, he was the only black who played with us for quite some time.

Now, to tell the truth, many of the players had resentment to the name Geezerball at first. Why? Many of the players were just too young to be called geezers, and the ones that were old enough to be called geezers, just did not want to admit it. Regardless, RJ Lomas created the name, and, as they say, the rest is history.

Geezerball has become a religion: Sunday for church and Saturday for basketball. Up to this day, a hundred and fifty or so players have joined the ranks of Geezerball: many of whom were white and many of whom were black, but, to tell the truth, nobody really cares. If you can play basketball, if you are not a whiner, if you love the game, you are welcome.

Besides Covington, Geezerball has been played at East Middle School in Farmington Hills where Seaborn was a Principal, at U of D Jesuit where RJ Lomas was the Admissions Director, at Shrine High School where RJ was an Administrator, at Our Lady Queen of Martyrs where RJ was coaching, at St. Hugo where Josh Daniels was coaching, at St. Regis where Josh was an Assistant Principal, at the Dietz-Trott Athletic Center where Mike Dietz is the Sports Management Director, and at Brother Rice High School where yours truly had worked for over thirty years.

During this time, our children would come and play down at the other end of the gym which provided great babysitting so that the dads could get a workout and the moms could be free of child care for those precious Saturday afternoon hours. Several of the children grew up while eagerly waiting to play with the big guys, the geezers, at the other end. Chad Seaborn, Gene's son, became a thorn in everyone's side, especially Milt Andrew's, who had to cover this youngster on a weekly basis. Derek Jones, whose father Al used to bring him during those early days at Covington, now is a regular at Geezerball.

My sons Jake and Josh and Nick have participated on Saturdays trying to surpass their old man. Begrudgingly, I must admit that day arrived a few years ago. Derek Palm has brought his two sons Denzel and DJ with DJ holding the record for the only one to ever dunk in a geezer game. Legend has it, though Derek won't admit it, that the dunk was against his own father!

What a special place and time! Geezerball is so much more than a place to play basketball. Geezerball was a place where new friendships were made and old friendships were strengthened. It was a place where learning to cooperate with a wide variety of people was expected. It was a place where egos had to be checked at the door. It was a place where we competed against each other ferociously but enjoyed each other immensely. It was a place where I met Thomas "Cookie" Marsh.

Truth be told, Marsh's reputation had entered the gym way before I actually greeted him. Little did I know back in 1970 when I first saw him playing basketball for the University of Detroit, that this star player who was on a totally different level from me – can you say Dean, the Dream Meminger – would become a teammate and a friend. Dean Meminger was the hotshot guard from Marquette University. Marquette was a national top ten team with Meminger leading their way. Marsh and the Titans defeated them on national television exposing Cookie Marsh as a potential NBA player and the Titans as a national power that year. Little did I know that this admired stranger would have me reflecting on and reminiscing about my upbringing, my reactions to major events, and my viewpoints on social issues.

When I first brought up the subject of writing a book together with Cookie, I was nervous about what his reaction would be. I already had the title in mind. We had just finished a Geezerball session and were in the locker room. Prior to popping this question, I had this burning inspiration to tell our story. I was haunted by the similarities we shared and by the importance of letting people know about them. As I was explaining my vision to him, I saw the bright light of understanding in Cookie's eyes as he kept nodding his head and interrupting me with his excited comments. He indicated that he always wanted to tell his story but did not know where to begin. He said that he was frustrated because he had so much to tell and no vehicle to let it escape. Cookie was not just in agreement, he was grateful for this opportunity. We resolved to begin this project without knowing exactly where it would lead.

That was about four years ago. In the interim, we learned more about each other: visiting one another's home, meeting wives and children, going to Cookie's Father's funeral, having conferences to discuss the project, and traveling together to Laurel, Mississippi to meet Cookie's relatives. In other words, we realized more and more that our parallel lives had truly intersected.

CHAPTER 2

The Early Days: The 1950s in Detroit

Thomas "Cookie" Marsh | black

My earliest recollection involved my mother walking me to school for the first time to kindergarten on the east side of Detroit, the Concord/Mt. Elliott area. Because my brother and older sisters had been through this journey before, I was not as scared as I might have been. I wanted to be a big boy and not cry, but I probably did when my mother left me. I quickly settled in.

The teacher took me by the hand and introduced me to the other kids, and we began doing what you do in kindergarten. At noon, my mother returned, and I was glad to see her mainly because I was going to go home and get something to eat. Kindergarten back then was just a half day.

My parents were great; my mother is still great being eighty-seven years old now. My father sadly died a couple of years ago. My mother reared us as my father worked – Chevrolet, Spring and Bumper Division.

Our family was a very close family. No, we did not sit down and eat meals together every day, but on Sundays and holidays we sure did. Everyone's schedule was hectic. The food would be prepared, so we would just grab something to eat on the go.

One incident that sticks in my memory from the Mt. Elliott days is what we still call today, "The Cat Incident." At the time, a lot of black families lived together with their cousins or other relatives in two family flats. We always lived with my cousins on my mother's side, her brother, my uncle and his kids. Anyway, a cat ended up scratching my cousin. We were very upset about it and made a vow that we were going to get back at this cat. We did the unthinkable.

My cousin and I went up on the top porch waiting for the cat to come out. We had gathered all these bricks and rocks, and we were going to stone the cat. So the cat came out and we let 'em go. Bombs away! The first brick hit the cat in the head and knocked it unconscious. We continued to bombard the cat until it was completely pulverized. We were both five or six years old, and our parents scared the bejesus out of us because they told us that this cat, having nine lives, was going to come back and scratch our eyeballs out. We were traumatized. Every night all we could dream about was this cat coming into the room, jumping on the bed and scratching our eyes out.

Now as we grew older, my cousin and I always have talked about this. Mary Bridges, now Dr. Bridges, is a psychiatrist, and I'm a social worker – can you figure that? A future psychiatrist and a future social worker actually killing this cat. The cat incident was very scary at that time.

Later on we moved to one of the two Detroit projects, the Jeffries, the other being Brewster famous for the celebrities, such as Diana Ross of the Supremes and Joe Louis the Heavyweight Champion of the World. The Jeffries on the west side had very few white people. This was a low income housing project.

We considered the Jeffries better than the Brewster because there wasn't much thuggish and violent behavior. So we moved to 1024 Temple Street in the Jeffries Project where I spent three to four years growing up. We didn't have a lot of playgrounds, so we made our own play areas, the alleys and the street. I didn't know anything about sports at the time. I wasn't into sports, just mostly games such as kick the can, hide and seek. We made our own toys since we only got toys at Christmas. We would make a whip or a top gun. We would take roller skates and make a pushcart or a go kart. My brother was the engineer, so to speak, as he knew how to design certain things and make these toys.

Growing up in the Jeffries Project, I then went to James Couzens Elementary School. Don't remember much, all black. Growing up here in Detroit, I didn't have much interaction with white people. My world consisted of a black world, a world where you only saw white people on TV in the commercials or on programs like *Leave it to Beaver* or *Sea Hunt*. We did see programs like *Little Rascals* that had two blacks: Stymie and Buckwheat- boy what names – Stymie and Buckwheat.

I had a good childhood; my mother made sure I was always clean and had everything we needed – never too much of what we wanted. We were a poor family, but, heck, I didn't know it until somebody told me. As I looked around, we had just as much as any other black family that was living in the Projects. I looked at my cousins; they had no more than what I had. But growing up at that time was a good time. I didn't have to worry about being molested or some adult snatching me or hurting me. I didn't have to worry about being shot or stabbed. Even our house being broken into wasn't a worry because there wasn't anything to steal. I mean we had nothing more than the person who would come in to steal. You couldn't get anything because we didn't have anything. Neighbors were pretty close. We did have a white family right next door to us, but, to my memory, we never played with those kids.

I remember looking out my window at the Lodge Expressway nearly every late afternoon watching the cars speed north after their owner's work in downtown Detroit. I loved cars. Anyone who has attended the Woodward Dream Cruise, the annual parade and display of vintage cars from the 1950s and 1960s, would understand my infatuation with these works of art. Besides enjoying these beautiful cars, I was, however, struck by another thought: all the drivers of these cars were white and were heading north out of our area. As a matter of fact, I came to the naïve conclusion that my father was the only black man who owned a car. Certainly no other black family in the Projects had a car.

After the Jeffries Project, we moved over to the west side of Detroit. We had to move from the Projects because they found out that my Dad was working for the factory and was making too much money. Prior to moving from the projects, we would go to the Eastern Market where we would buy fruit and vegetables and live poultry, chickens.

I remember being actually traumatized by my parents bringing a live chicken home that I thought would be a new pet. I actually had thought up a name for it. Then, my mother and father started ringing that chicken's neck while I was watching until the neck snapped off. Then I viewed the chicken running around for a few seconds splattering blood everywhere then falling over dead. Can you imagine what that felt like or looked like to a kid? Yea, I was traumatized. Needless to say, I did not want to eat chicken for a long time. I certainly couldn't eat that chicken that night for supper thinking what had happened to it. Later, I found out that this is just something black families did. My parents weren't the only ones wringing chickens' necks.

All this came from my parents' upbringing in the South. And we traveled to the South every summer when we would get out of school. Most times my father would drive us down, and then come back to Detroit until he had his vacation or what they called "changeover" in the factory for the new models. Then he would come back down there and take his two weeks' vacation, and then we would all travel back to Detroit. Now, I was born in Laurel, Mississippi but reared in Detroit. I thought that being reared in Mississippi and raised in Detroit gave me a good balance. I was able to witness segregation and discrimination being thrust upon us from the North and certainly from the South.

When we went to the South, we were black persons who had to abide by the way it was there. So we would travel from Detroit to Mississippi and watch the marches. Along the highway, I remember seeing the "colored" signs: "For Coloreds Only", "For Whites Only" in terms of the water fountains and restrooms. As we traveled, we couldn't stop and eat meals once we got south of Cincinnati. You have to remember that this trip was over a thousand miles. My mother would cook our food for the entire trip, fried chicken, sweet potato pie, lunch meat, crackers, and a jug of Kool-Aid to drink. We could not stop to eat because we were in what you would call the "Jim Crowe" law land. This was a time when segregation was actually a law.

I remember, though, just how good the trip and those meals were. I can still almost smell and taste the chicken all wrapped up in the bread to absorb the grease. It was delicious. Mind you, I was really not a chicken fan as I already explained why but I kind of forgot about that and ate the food. There was no air conditioning in the car as we drove down there as my Daddy didn't believe in air conditioning. He said if you are hot, roll down the window. I think he called it "armstrong" air conditioning. If your arm was strong enough to roll down the window (no power windows in those days) then you would have air conditioning of sorts. That's how we got our air conditioning. He finally got an air conditioned car in 1973. As we would travel up and down that highway, it became a big deal. It was something that we looked forward to.

My parents would try to explain to us the best that they could what the race relations were and the law in Mississippi at the time. They explained about their experiences as they grew up in the South as kids. Certainly, we did not experience that overt segregation here in Detroit at that time. In Detroit the segregation and discrimination was more covert. In Mississippi, it was overt.

From the time that he car rolled into the dirt driveway of my Grandmother's home, we ran! Wide open spaces, grass, dirt roads, and a loving family everywhere we looked. The only sounds we heard were birds chirping and the family laughing together. Here, I saw cows and chickens. I rode on the back of a wagon pulled by two mules. I learned to drive a car as I drove down a dirt country road. I learned of my roots from my great-grandmother. What a difference from inner city Detroit with its sirens and honking and car engines.

Curiously, because my cousins were poorer than we were, we felt rich. Heck, we had shoes on our feet; they didn't. Momma always kept us clean and in good clothes despite the fact that they came from the Goodwill second-hand store. Oddly, back in Detroit, I never felt poor because no one had any more than we did, yet here, everyone had less.

Down there, prejudice was always looking at us straight in the face, literally, and raised its ugly head on several occasions. To say that prejudice was overt would be accurate. Truly though, I really did not notice it until years later upon reflection. I was just a kid, and even though I encountered discrimination, I just rolled with it. A child does not know any better and can not possibly comprehend the magnitude of these unfair discrepancies.

The name of our relatives' road was blasphemed into "Big Nigger Road." Ironically, the real name of the road was "Friendship Road." Go figure. Though curious, I did not understand the implication until years later.

FRIENDSHIP ROAD

One summer day, all of us were going to what we called "To Town." Black people would travel to the one section that they could do their shopping. My southern cousin went on ahead coming upon this restaurant which was not in the black section. He stopped at the doorway, but I went in and sat at a stool at the counter wanting to get a milkshake.

Just as an aside, my Mother had all of us dressed nicely. My shoeless cousin, a country boy, was very happy to go with us. Down there the kids went barefoot. Of course, we didn't. We had nice shoes on and new to us clothes; most of them were second hand but nice and clean. I felt good and confident in myself.

So as I was saying, my cousin and I wandered down that little street called Front Street, and I went into the restaurant. I noticed that when I went in, he stayed at the door. He just stood at the door looking down. Well, me being from Up North, not knowing really about segregation and that kind of stuff, I went on in to the restaurant and started spinning around on the stool and started playing. I kind of noticed that there were all white folks in there, but I still didn't pay too much attention to it.

Come to think of it now, the other patrons in the diner had these odd looks on their faces that could be summed up in one word: disbelief! How could a "nigra" be invading our restaurant? Again, as I think back on the situation from an older person's perspective, these white folks probably thought that I was part of some movement or demonstration.

Perhaps they were bracing themselves for more "nigras" to be entering their restaurant. I again looked over to my cousin in the obligatory stance that blacks had to assume when in the presence of white people back then hands clasped in front of his stomach and his eyes glued to the floor.

MISSISSIPPI DINER

The lady at the counter came over to me, the waitress, and she didn't say it in a mean or vicious or angry way but she did talk to me as I was a child, "You know, we don't serve niggers here." I still didn't know what she was talking about, so I replied, "I don't want any niggers; I want a milkshake." She kind of chuckled knowing that I didn't understand and then said it again, "I'm sorry, but we don't serve niggers here." The second time I caught on, not to the part about the niggers, but to the part "we don't serve." So I knew what that meant so I kind of got up and started walking out.

Well by this time, the people had found my mother where she was shopping and told her, "Your son done went into that all-white restaurant down there, and he's in there." She dropped everything that she was doing and ran down Front Street. By this time my cousin and I were walking down the street, and she reached and grabbed me and looked at me making sure I was all right. Then she looked at my cousin and said, "You are going to get the whuppin' of your life." I couldn't understand why he was going to get a whuppin' because I was the one who entered the diner, not he, but later on I did understand. It was because he knew better- he lived down there. He knew how it was, but he still allowed me to go in there.

During this time period in the South, my "invasion" of the diner could have resulted in something very, very bad for me and him because they had actually lynched black people in the South for doing exactly what I'd just done.

Some of you reading this might remember the Emmett Till incident where a black kid growing up in Chicago went to the South and while he was down there allegedly said something inappropriate to a white lady. As a result he was lynched. I could have been another Emmett Till, but I thank God that I wasn't.

I also remember going to the movies in Mississippi where we had to go in the side door and couldn't sit downstairs where the white people were. We had to sit upstairs, far away from the movie screen and, of course, the white people. When we went swimming, we could not swim with white people. They would actually drain the pool after we swam, so the next day there would be fresh, clean water for the white people. They'd drain the pool saying white people should not have to swim in the same water that black people had been in. Three days for each race and one day for draining and cleaning. That was the South's version of equality. You may also remember the segregation of schools back then. I never experienced that in the South because we were rarely down there during the school year.

However, come to think of it, my schooling in the North was segregated perhaps not by law but by actuality. Neighborhood schools were either in all black neighborhoods or all white neighborhoods. I remember that later on in the 1970s or 1980s the City of Detroit instituted a bussing plan for school integration. Truly, it was a little late because the city had become predominantly black, so the black kids were being bussed to other schools that were predominantly black. Go figure. For me, until college, I never went to school with a white student.

Occasionally we would head to Mississippi at Christmas when the car factories would shut down. I remember another incident around Christmas time when it was a tradition to shoot off fireworks, completely different from the North where it was cold. In Detroit, we didn't set off fireworks at Christmas, only around July 4th or other summer events. Down in the South, you could have an eighty degree day in December, so the fireworks tradition was not strange for them.

Anyway, we were at my grandmother's house. I will never forget this group of white, young kids driving by and throwing these cherry bombs which were a type of fireworks but very loud and could be very dangerous-hammerheads. You may not know what I'm talking about, but they were very dangerous which had a powerful punch with a loud explosion. They would come by taunting us, and my uncle, who was sixteen or seventeen at the time, said that we were not going to allow them to keep doing this to us because it was very upsetting to my grandmother. So he armed us with bricks and sticks and bottles and said when they come back again, they are going to get what they need to get. So we lay down in the ditch beside the road in front of the house, and when that car came back again, we unloaded on them. We threw bricks and bottles and broke their windows and dented up their cars. They sped off, and surprisingly, we never saw them or heard them or heard about them again. This was a very vivid memory.

But also, there were some good times in the South. Being with family was most important to me. Seeing my parents, who had sacrificed so much to move to the North, being so very happy to be reunited with their kinfolk made me feel good. I had a chance to see what it was like in the country or rural area as opposed to being in an urban setting in the city. I had never seen so much grass and so many trees. I felt blessed that I had an upbringing in both settings.

I never had any racial incidents living in the city of Detroit. As I said previously, I lived in a black world. It was not until late in high school that I actually had any contact with a white person.

We were down there once a year, and as the segregation laws were abolished things began to change- some. There was always that underlying attitude of white folks not really accepting blacks, and there were blacks who did not want to accept any whites. You had blacks who thought that all white people were bad.

But there is one thing that I've grown to know in life: there are two kinds of people in this world: good and evil. And you have that in both races. You have good white people, and you have good black people. You have bad white people, and you have bad black people. So I grew up with that in mind, and that's what my parents always taught me. There's good and there's bad.

As I grew older, and I started to get involved in sports around 1959-1960, we moved from the Jeffries Projects over to our very first house, a house that we weren't renting but were actually buying. And I remember my mother being so happy about having a house where her kids would have a backyard to play in and where she could plant a little garden. We had an apple tree in the backyard. We had a garage to put our car in. The neighborhood was on the west side of Detroit on a street called Lee Place, 1434 Lee Place. I will always remember that.

It was a time when a lot of Jewish people had lived in that area and had started moving out when blacks started moving in. And as they say, oops, there goes the neighborhood. But it didn't happen like that. The blacks that were homeowners, we took care of our place where we lived and our community. We cleaned our own streets; we swept in front of our own house, and the neighbors cleaned in front of theirs. Everybody did that; it was a very nice place to live.

One of the things that made it great for me is that we had a Boys Club. The Boys Club did so much for me in terms of growing up and introducing me to sports and having a positive place to go where we had adult supervision. I must mention Mr. Kennedy who was a leader and mentor at the Boys Club. He was a very special man to me. Sure, I had my father, but I believe that all of us need someone else to help guide us.

Hearing the same words of wisdom that we heard from our fathers often takes on a deeper meaning when we hear it from someone else who we also respect. Of course we had our playgrounds, and playgrounds are great in the summertime, but in the winter time there was little to do.

I remember that the city would come with heavy plowing equipment to push dirt into a large rectangle and fill it with water and call it an ice pond. Well, shit, an ice pond! What did we know about an ice pond? What were we supposed to do with it? Nobody had ice skates; maybe one or two kids did. So we ended up just basically throwing rocks and sticks on to the pond and watching it freeze. Then we would get out on it and run around and try not to fall as we slid around. That was it.

But the Boys Club offered so much more. We had an arts and crafts room; we had a library; we had a gym. We had the adult supervision. The whole experience was structured. Girls were not allowed at that time. This was strictly the boys club. You have some notable individuals that came up through the Boys Club all across the country. The one that comes to mind is Denzel Washington.

Denzel, famous actor, was a Boys Club boy. He often talks about his wonderful experiences there.

There were wonderful experiences year round. My momma knew that if I wasn't at home or school that I was at the Boys Club. She knew the supervisors especially Mr. Carl Woods who was a tremendous mentor and eventually left to go to St. Louis to open up a state of the art Boys Club there. The Boys Club took us to Harsens Island, Michigan for a camping trip. All I could think of when I was out in the woods there is 'where is the cee-ment?' We also had what was called the May Festival. So many activities occurred during this time, but the one that stands out was the dance. This was the only time that girls were allowed into the Boys Club.

Like I said, growing up we didn't have much, but always what we needed! I remember this one time I asked my dad for a new pair of basketball shoes. Every player who called himself a basketball player was wearing Converse All-Stars, the Chuck Taylor model. I did not have any. I asked my Daddy to get some for me. He was working out at the Livonia plant and would pass this shoe store every day on his way home. "Run Faster and Jump Higher with Your P F Flyers" "Nope, not those shoes, Daddy, no PF Flyers for me." The next day he comes back with Beta Bullets after returning the Flyers. "Nope, not those shoes, Daddy." Then next day he comes back with U. S. Keds after returning the Beta Bullets. "Nope, not those either, Daddy, I want the Chucks." Being very patient up until this time, Daddy says, "I ain't spending no ten dollars on a pair of basketball shoes." And that was that. So I am playing at the Boys Club, and a young man about three years older than I said, "Cookie, you are going to be wearing Converse All-Stars. With that, Julius Purfory took off his Chucks and gave them to me. Of course they were three sizes too big but with enough pairs of socks, I was styling in my Chucks.

Thomas "Whitey" Daniels | *white*

4610, 4640, 4628 Van Dyke Avenue, Detroit, Michigan (before zip codes) as East Side as it gets. Walking to Belle Isle was easy; however, the two to three mile walk often became longer due to the avoidance of stray dogs and fearful people. Back in those days, they would call it a mixed neighborhood, a euphemism for the n-----s were moving in, as the primarily German, Italian, and Polish neighbors moved out being replaced by the Negroes. As a child, what did I care? As long as you didn't whine, as long as you didn't think you were better than the rest of us, as long as you loved to play, you were welcome.

VAN DYKE AVENUE

Unfortunately, that wasn't the case with many of the adults who fled the area or cursed the changing environment if not openly then in the privacy of their aging homes and viewpoints. What starts with an "n" and ends with an "r" that you never want to call a black person? Neighbor!

Louie Betka, Chuckie Mavros, and David Henze (*white boys*) blended in with Gregory Mays, Marvin Culver and Winfred Didlake (*black boys*) until all the white families moved out including us. My father made the pronouncement, probably at my mother's (a native of North Carolina) urging. We were moving "way out" to Gratiot and McNichols (Six Mile).

The plan was for me and my sister to attend the all-white Catholic Assumption Grotto Grade School. Almost-Mary was accepted; I wasn't – the 8th grade classes were too full. So I continued my academic and social education at St. Catherine's at Maxwell and Sylvester. Bob, my brother, would be taking busses to the University of Detroit High School.

EAGLE DAIRY ICE CREAM

Two racist incidents stayed with me over the years.

The first one involved my dear mother who, of course, was influenced by her upbringing in North Carolina. Because basketball practice for the 8th grade team at St. Catherine's did not start until 5:00 p.m. each day, I had to find something to do and somewhere to go for ninety minutes after school. The Didlakes, Winfred and Donald, had a few of us over to their home to wait it out. I really enjoyed being with them and their hospitality. My mother became aware of my whereabouts after school and commanded me not to go to their house because they were black. I know that God has forgiven me for being disobedient.

The other incident was with my Uncle Gene, another Southerner who was visiting us one summer, sternly warning me never to go swimming with Negroes. Cock a doodle doo! I told him that I would never do such a thing. See you at the Belle Isle Beach, the Pingree Park wading pool, and the Lipke pool. Oh well, another lie on my part. Lord, have mercy!

Early on I learned , just like with any other race, there were good blacks and bad blacks. I am pleased that even at a very young age I knew the difference. There were the bad blacks that jumped my brother and me on Forest Avenue by the Korash Florist. What a terrifying incident that was.

We were coming back from a summer job that we had tending to an old lady's yard getting ten cents per hour. We had just been paid our sixty cents apiece. We were not only fearful of getting beaten up, but also of being robbed of our hard-earned pay. I ran as fast as I could and ended up on someone's front porch calling for help. No one was home, so I continued to run home as fast as I could. I was not followed. To this day, I think I should have stayed there with my brother, but I didn't. After I was home for what seemed an eternity, Bob comes strolling into the house without a scratch and still possessing his sixty cents. There was a man, perhaps his Guardian Angel, reading a newspaper in his parked car along Forest Avenue. The man motioned for Bob to enter the car escaping the trouble. Whew!

Another incident was the bad black kid who stole my baseball glove but who paid the price as Ricky Johnson, one of the big guys in our neighborhood, chased him down on his bike and returned the glove to a happy but tearful me. Although I got my glove back, I learned a stern lesson from my father who was sent looking for me because I did not return home when the noon church bells rang signaling me to go home. The church bells were not to be ignored!

Always I would be walking in the door to our home approximately ten minutes after the last bell was clanged. My father's unsympathetic but true words still resound with me today. "If you had been coming home on time, none of this would have happened."

And, of course, there were all the bad black kids who attended Barbour School. To this day, the mention of Barbour School sends cold shivers down my spine. Truly, I never had proof that these public school students were delinquents. Sometimes rumors just get handed down from one year to the next. To strengthen these conceptions, St. Catherine's Grade School adjusted its schedule to let us out earlier than the Barbour School dismissal. None of us would misbehave in class risking having to stay after school and meeting not only the wrath of our parents but also the danger of Barbour School students.

BARBOUR SCHOOL

Every now and then a rumor would knife through the school about an impending rumble. Even the black students at St. Catherine were fearful. Regretfully, I never met a Barbour School student to relieve this perception. Perhaps through this book, I will. Looking back from the vantage point of older age and experience, I am sorry that I had these unfounded perceptions.

The good blacks as I mentioned before were the Didlakes. I was very upset that Winfred did not attend U of D High School with me. He decided to stay at St.Catherine. Also, Marvin Culver was another great black friend. He and I were in Boy Scouts together and actually went to Belle Isle to fulfill some requirements for a badge. I still remember our satisfaction in starting a fire there in order to have a cookout. The Polish sausages were delicious. We built this fire in a wooded, remote area of the island. It is a wonder that we did not burn down any of that forest.

Regardless, through sports and games and schooling, I knew the difference between good and evil. I knew that the color of a person's skin wasn't what made this difference. In fact, the black Rudolph brothers were a great example. Although brothers, they were quite different. Timmy, my age, although an instigator, always was a good kid and playmate during lunch hour on the playground. Gary, his brother, was a different story. He had a chip on his shoulder, and even though he was a year younger, thought he could intimidate me and others. Finally, I had enough of him after months of patience. Needless to say, he never messed with me again.

The 1950s were, for the most part, a carefree time, leaving the house in the morning, coming back when the noon (Angelus) church bells began to ring, playing around the house all afternoon, having dinner at exactly 4:00 so my father could go to his bar tending job by 5:00, and then playing in the neighborhood until the street lights came on which beckoned us home.

Baseball and softball were big at that time. I would go to the field with high hopes that the big guys would choose me to play. Sometimes I would be chosen and would play right field, a direction no one hit the ball. Sometimes the big guys would have mercy on me and roll the ball to home plate so that I could hit it. One time I smashed it all the way on the ground, of course, to the school some 200 feet away. The big guys took notice, and my confidence swelled. I knew then and there that I could become a very good baseball player, leading me to a small scholarship to play on the baseball team at the University of Detroit-more on that later.

Getting back to the playground, because there were not always enough players to have nine or ten on a side, often we would have a designated catcher (probably the worst or youngest player, often me) and the right side of the field would be out because we did not have enough players to have a second baseman or a right fielder. In other words, if you hit the ball to the right of second base, you would automatically be out. Do you now see why the big guys let me play right field? I was the only one of the group who threw right and batted left. If I hit the ball to right field, I would automatically be out. Therefore, I developed an uncanny ability to hit the ball to left field which served me quite well as I continued with my baseball/softball career.

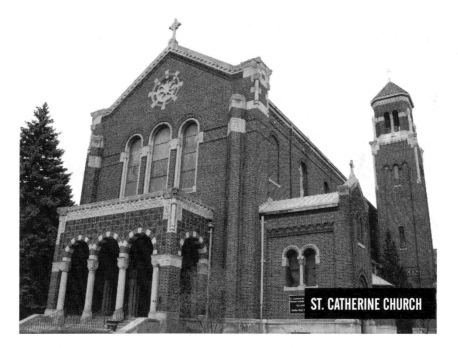

ST. CATHERINE CHURCH

Another curiosity about growing up was the lack of injuries to any of us. Certainly we had the skinned knees and bumps and bruises from "pom, pom peteaway." This was a rough game that placed one kid in the middle of the rock and glass covered playground with the other kids starting against the fence. The object was for all the kids to get across to the other side of the playground without the kid in the middle tackling them. If you were tackled, then you became the ally of the kid in the middle. The game would be played until only one person remained untackled. Then that person would be the winner who got to be the initial tackler for the next game. Can you imagine what we looked like and smelled like when we returned to our afternoon classes at St. Catherine Elementary School?

There were just three injuries to me of any significance. Two of the three can be attributed to Spider, my older brother. This nickname was given by Louie Betka who probably was looking through the *National Geographic* for bare-chested African women when he stumbled across a picture of a spider monkey that had a striking resemblance to my gangly brother Bob. The nickname has stuck to this day. I had mentioned that the youngest player would sometimes be the designated catcher at our ball games. The designated catcher was nothing more than a breathing backstop, but, hey, I was happy to be included.

Anyway, Spider inadvertently hit me just under my left eye with his follow through of the bat. Blood was gushing everywhere mixed with my salty tears. I walked the five blocks home by myself to be comforted and attended to by my dear mother; certainly, no doctor would be consulted-couldn't afford it. Perhaps we went over to Mr. Rose who was the pharmacist across the street who acted as a surrogate doctor. By the way, Spider finished his at bat and did not take me home. Who could blame him? It was the last inning of a very close game!

Another injury that I sustained came as the result of a hot game of "kick the can" or "release the bell room" or maybe just "tag." I cannot remember for a good reason as you will see. Trying to not get caught or captured or to be "It", I decided to crawl over the railing on the porch and jump to safety before Spider caught me. Unfortunately, my foot got caught in the railing rungs. I crashed head first into the waiting cement. In retrospect, I can't say what hurt worse. Was it the throbbing pain from the awful lump I had on my forehead or the fact that I was captured? The game always went on.

The third injury occurred not in a game but by being intrigued by a tree being cut down along Maxwell Avenue just south of Manila Street near Germaine's Party Store. Germaine's had the coldest Sweet Sixteen pop you could ever imagine. His ice filled coolers were numbingly cold as I would fish around for a Rock-n-Rye whenever I was fortunate to have a dime in my pocket. Not looking where I was going and running because I did not want to be late to my afternoon session at school and have to be detained which would cause me to face the Barbour School gang, I did not see the kid with a wagon coming just as fast toward me. Seriously, I think I broke my shin. That thing throbbed for weeks. Again, no doctor was seen-couldn't afford it. I also did not tell my parents and risk getting yelled at for almost being late to school.

No haunted houses, no skeletons, no goblins were needed. Halloween of 1954 was scary enough without them. P-O-L-I-O! These five letters scared the life out of people who grew up at that time before Doctor Jonas Salk's miraculous vaccination.

Halloween in 1954 started out as a great time, trick or treating through the neighborhood. One of our treats from "begging" at Halloween was pumpkin seeds. These white, salty treats also could be bought at Menino's Party Store for a nickel a bag. To this day when I think of pumpkin seeds, I associate them with what follows. Bob, my brother, took ill able to barely walk to get to the bathroom. In those days, it was not uncommon for the doctor to come to the house. Dr. Lentine examined Bob there on the couch and turned to my parents and stated, "I suspect your son has polio." At the time, my mother pointed her finger to pumpkin seeds as the cause, far-fetched for sure, but because she was scared to death, her logic had left her. Needless to say, we threw the remainder of the pumpkin seeds out, and I never had any more that she knew about. The ramifications of this dreaded disease ranged from permanent paralysis of the limbs, to the inability to breathe having to be in an iron lung, to death.

Polio was no joke. We all were scared to death. My mother was pregnant with my sister Mary as we all wondered who would be next to get this contagious disease. Bob went immediately to Herman Kiefer Hospital in Detroit for treatment. We waited, waited to see what devastation the disease would inflict on Bob and waited to see if any of us would contract the disease. Fortunately, Bob recovered with just some lifelong muscular effects, and none of us got sick. Most people, mostly young, were not that fortunate.

Truly, though, the 1950's were innocent years. Although on paper we were dirt poor, I always had enough food and care. It was a time when neighbors watched out for us. Never was there a worry that we would be kidnapped or abused in any way. I was always filthy from playing hard and exhausted from long, active days. No one had to tell me twice to go to bed. I often fell asleep on the living room floor watching *Sea Hunt* or *Hockey Night in Canada*. Even on Saturday nights I tried to stay up to watch *Shock Theater* but to no avail.

We never had air conditioning in any of our flats along Van Dyke or on Pelkey. The only fan we had seemed to be always pointed at my father who wore an old handkerchief around his neck claiming that he had a hole under his chin that continued to drip sweat. Who could argue with that logic? No one did, so he continued to hog the fan. Along with the stifling heat, the 98.6 degrees that permeated from my brother as we shared the same bed didn't help matters.

The bed, however, is where I learned that rules are rules, never to be broken without consequences. An imaginary line divided the bed vertically. If any one of us crossed that line, an inevitable kick would send the offender back to his ordained place without complaint. Rules were rules!

I always liked the fall except for a huge interruption called school. "Two Hand Touch" street football was our game. I loved it because we could play it with as few as three people. Therefore, Spider and I had only to find one more person. As you might imagine, Spider was a terrific receiver. He frustrated me to no end as he was taller and lankier than I was. There was very little I could do to prevent him from catching the ball. How we didn't break off car antennas and side view mirrors is beyond me.

Winter back then had its own intrigue. I remember taking a long time to bundle up to go outside only to get a face washing or a snowball in the face and scurrying back into the house after just a few minutes outside. I really never liked the winter and still don't except for playing and coaching basketball. However, that sport was non-existent for me until seventh grade. More on that later.

"Good Packing" was the phrase that would excite any kid at that time. Now we could build a snowman, a fort, or have a great snowball fight. Sometimes we would play street hockey, certainly not on skates but with our heavy multiple buckle boots. It seemed getting prepared to play took more time than the game itself especially with all the interruptions caused by cars coming down the side street on Norvel. How dare those drivers use our street! What were they thinking?

When spring arrived, love was certainly in the air, my love of baseball. I had to oil up the old three-fingered Stan Musial model glove. For my birthday one year, my dear father relented and bought me a Charley Maxwell model that was about eleven dollars. I will never forget that trip (walk, we never had a car) with dad to East Side Sporting Goods on Van Dyke near Harper. I loved Charley Maxwell, nickname of Paw-Paw due to the town he was from outside of Kalamazoo, Michigan. Maxwell, a Detroit Tiger outfielder, had an uncanny ability of hitting a home run on every Sunday. I was so thrilled with that glove until some brat in the neighborhood told me that Charley Maxwell was left handed. How could that be a Charley Maxwell glove when it was right handed?

We had a very organized softball league run by the Dads' Club of St. Catherine Parish. There was a draft of players and different levels of competition according to age. One of my fondest memories was of Albert Marshall's father, a black man, who attended every one of our games. He would stand along the fence and cheer for all of us even shouting at the opposing players," He ain't nothin' but a ham." He was one of the black lives that mattered to me back then.

I have to add a few stories about what it was like being taught by nuns in a Catholic grade school. The stories are legendary. I remember the day Gregory May's mother came to school probably at the bidding of the dear nun that taught our class. To say the least, Gregory was a handful, not a bad kid but shall we say behaviorally challenged. Today he would have been labeled with ADD or ADHD and been on medication. When Gregory's mother entered the room just after the beginning of the school, we were all in rapt attention. Parents never entered the sacrosanct domain of the teacher. This was third grade, I believe. We immediately noticed that she had a rubber hose, the kind you would see attached to a ringer washing machine. Oh boy! Did she let Gregory have it!

Another incident was told to me by Mike McKeon, a good friend who attended Redford St. Mary Grade School. This time it was sixth grade and during a fire drill. When the nuns said line up single file in a straight line without talking, they meant it. Unfortunately, one of the boys couldn't resist the stray dog that had infiltrated the line outside the school. A blue and white blur with a closed fist was seen running down the line of students. POW!!! Right in the mouth of the unsuspecting, "disobedient" dog lover.

Don't throw snowballs around school!! What were they thinking? Another Catholic grade school put a quick stop to snowball fights. A great packing snow fell one morning, and all the kids couldn't wait for the lunch hour to get outside. They had a great time with the first snowfall of the season. Upon entering the school for the afternoon session, a slow- moving line developed. Stationed at each entry were two nuns with metal rulers. Each student, regardless if they participated in the snow throwing or not, was given four swats with the ruler, one on each side of each hand. Ouch! especially if your hands were ice cold due to throwing snowballs. After the students had entered school and returned to their rooms, the Pastor got on the P.A. to announce that there certainly would never be any more snow throwing around the school. Duh!

In many ways, I lived a charmed life in the 1950's. So much of what I have become as a man had its roots back then.

Speaking of roots, I also had relatives in the South on my Mother's side, North Carolina. As did Cookie with Mississippi, I loved the opportunity to travel to North Carolina, but my reactions were somewhat different from Cookie's.

I certainly felt poor when we were down there, not because anyone overtly drew my attention to that fact, but because I noticed things. My relatives were well off living in beautiful homes which they owned in wonderful neighborhoods with well cared for parks nearby. I too was amazed by the wide open spaces found in the neighborhoods of Winston-Salem and Elkin. My Grandmother had a large park at the end of her street where she lived at 714 Bellvue. My cousins Vicki, Debbi, Patsy, and Ann wore fine clothes, took swimming lessons, and had all the advantages of the rich.

However, the greatest advantage provided by these trips was to see a different side of life. The world was not Van Dyke and Forest, east side of Detroit. On our trek down at a time before the major freeways had been built, my Great Aunt Florence and Great Uncle Roy showed me scenery and sights of America that I would never otherwise have seen as we traveled through Ohio, West Virginia, and Tennessee.

When I was in grade school, I had to memorize all the state capitals, but now a few of them came alive like Charleston, West Virginia and Columbus, Ohio. They would always make sure to show me highlights like the State Capitol buildings that, I am sure, they had seen many, many times before. I am forever grateful for that experience.

Going to North Carolina lit a fire in me that showed me that I could be much more than my childhood environment. As a matter of fact, when I got home, I began to see things in their stark reality. I realized that where we lived was quite shabby, old, and dirty. I know that my parents were providing the best that they knew how, so I am not condemning them, far from it.

As soon as I got home, I clearly remember that I started to clean out certain messes around the home trying to emulate the southern relatives' houses. Being eleven or twelve, I believe that sudden burst of cleaning energy only lasted so long.

Therefore, as experienced by Cookie, I too felt better about myself and my place in the world. I too had deep roots that no matter how far away by time and distance would remain strong.

CHAPTER 3
The 60s and High School Years

Thomas "Cookie" Marsh | *black*

Now, this is no brag; this is just fact. I was a great shooter, probably one of the best around. I was a high school All-American. I was recruited by over a hundred different colleges. I wanted to stay close to home, so I decided to stay in Detroit, but my high school coach wanted me to go to Bowling Green, Ohio.

Mo Blackwell who was a great athlete who attended Holy Redeemer and then went on to play football, basketball and baseball at Wayne State University in Detroit, told me that when he and his teammates would be shooting around in the gym in high school that they would try to emulate me calling out "Cookie Marsh" when they made a long shot. Mo was another white guy that I met indirectly through geezerball.

Let me go back to high school. Playing in the Detroit Public Schools League at that time, we had schools that were not considered inner city schools. These schools had predominantly white players like Denby, Finney, Osborne, Cody, and Redford. So this was the first time I actually started playing against white kids.

Now we had something like that with the Boys Club because we would travel to different parts of the State. If you won your tournament championship here in the city, then you may go some place like Bay City, all white at that time.

But again, the one thing about athletics is that if you were good, you were good. It didn't make any difference if you were black or white. You quickly learned to respect individuals not by the color of their skin but by how good could they play and what type of athlete they were. And I think it worked both ways.

In 1967, I got invited to a basketball camp and golf school combination. It was up in Oscoda, Michigan. Most of the kids there were white because they played golf. I didn't know anything about golf. We played golf because my high school basketball coach was the golf coach, and he couldn't get any of us black guys to play golf, so he asked the basketball players to be a part of this golf team. So, I did.

What should have been a culture shock for me really wasn't. We, blacks and whites, were there for the same purpose, so what did it matter what anyone looked like? That camp had just one other black kid who later on in life crossed paths with me because he went to Central Michigan University and played basketball, and I went to the University of Detroit and played basketball. When we played against each other, we would talk about that experience up there in Oscoda. Again, I still didn't have a lot of interaction with whites. In 1969 I went to the University of Detroit, and for the very first time I am living in the same room with a white kid, Joe Sabourin, great guy. I only stayed on campus for maybe a half a year because after that I was married and then lived off-campus. I was actually going to school and raising a family. I had a white coach whereas before every coach I ever had was black with the exception of my junior high basketball coach Sam Taub, legendary coach at Detroit Mumford. He was an alumnus of the University of Detroit and had played basketball there. It was ironic that I played for the city championship against Mumford and that same Coach Sam Taub in 1969. I was playing for Detroit Northern. He said that nobody, when they asked him how they were going to contain me, contains him, and nobody stops him. No brag, just fact: I was averaging over thirty points per game. I was shooting nothing but 3s, but they didn't have a three point line back then. If the three point line had been down, I may have averaged 50 to 60 points per game. But he said, "No, we're not going to stop him; we'll just try to contain his teammates and slow them down." They ended up beating us for the city championship, something that I was deeply hurt by, but I knew that we gave it our best shot. We were undersized; they had a big team with center Marvin Taylor at 6'9."

The 60s were a fabulous time for me. They were a time that I found my identity and a time when I began to understand how the world really worked, how the political and racial situation was within the United States, and just how each one of those subjects impacted me as a young, black kid growing up on the west side of Detroit. I am sure my story is similar to a lot of other individuals who were growing up in other urban areas, lower economic situations, parents who were doing the very best they could to make sure we had what we needed not necessarily what we wanted, but certainly provided us with everything we needed. So with that being said, I just want this to be known that the 60s was a transitional time for me, but it was a good time. I actually met my wife Annette in the 60s. We started dating in junior high school, 1963. And here it is 2016 and we are still a part of each other's lives. Now, how she put up with me all that time, I will never know because truly, truly, she is my better half.

The music defined the 60s. The music defined where you were as a teenager. The only music that I knew about was the music that was coming out of Motown and also some Blues singers. My parents were raised in southern Mississippi, and they listened to a lot of Blues which translated into what we heard around the house as kids: B.B. King, spiritual/gospel like the Dixie Boys and the Five Blind Boys. These were groups and individuals who were large in the spiritual music, such as Mahalia Jackson and a number of others that I got accustomed to listening to.

My mother was a church going mother: she made sure that we got to church every Sunday. My Dad sang in the choir, the male chorus. As we grew up, my brother and sisters got involved in the young adult choir, but somehow, some way I never did. It always seemed that when I got old enough to join, they would up the age. I may be paranoid, but I think it had something to do with my inability to really sing because I couldn't carry a note in a large bucket.

But we were there every Sunday in church. Therefore, a lot of my upbringing had to do with what I learned in church. It was not so much about spirituality but about doing the right and wrong things in life. I truly believe that my spiritual connection and relationship with God have anchored me into a life that would not allow me to waver too far. It allowed me to be rooted to something, so I am thankful for that.

Of course, that great sound from the Motown was the thing that was being put down all around. It was Motown, baby! Motown crossed into whites, blacks, Hispanics, purples, blues, or greens. It did not make any difference. You were just on the scene when you were with the Motown theme. I loved Motown, growing up within blocks of the Motown studio, I got a chance to meet and interact with Smokey Robinson and David Ruffin. These were individuals that I not only saw on TV but stood in awe in there presence. I also remember one of my mentors Roger Chandler, nickname "Peanut", Cass Tech, student-athlete, played in the band, played basketball, baseball, football. He was older than I and one of my mentors through the Boys Club. Peanut ended up playing bass guitar for Eddie Kendricks, former Temptation.

We had a mixture of music during that time. Tom Daniels recently showed me a top thirty music chart put out in 1963 by a popular radio station WKNR. Mind you, this was a chart mixing all the popular types of music at the time. There were thirteen black singers/groups in the top thirty with Dionne Warwick at the top with "Anyone Who Had a Heart."

I listened to CKLW, a radio station out of Windsor, Ontario, Canada and Detroit's own WXYZ with Lee Allen on the horn. These courageous stations and disc jockeys played a variety of music as the black artists were just breaking through into the mainstream of American life. Two music and dance oriented shows were Swingin'Time hosted by a famous disc jockey Robin Seymour and, of course, American Bandstand with Dick Clark. Although we looked at the kind of dancing they

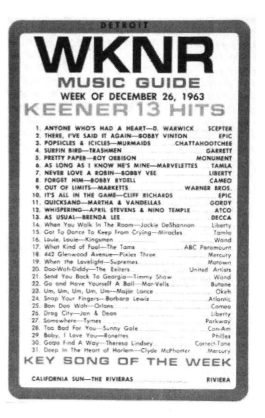

DETROIT

WKNR

MUSIC GUIDE
WEEK OF DECEMBER 26, 1963
KEENER 13 HITS

1. ANYONE WHO'S HAD A HEART—D. WARWICK   SCEPTER
2. THERE, I'VE SAID IT AGAIN—BOBBY VINTON   EPIC
3. POPSICLES & ICICLES—MURMAIDS   CHATTAHOOTCHEE
4. SURFIN BIRD—TRASHMEN   GARRETT
5. PRETTY PAPER—ROY ORBISON   MONUMENT
6. AS LONG AS I KNOW HE'S MINE—MARVELETTES   TAMLA
7. NEVER LOVE A ROBIN—BOBBY VEE   LIBERTY
8. FORGET HIM—BOBBY RYDELL   CAMEO
9. OUT OF LIMITS—MARKETTS   WARNER BROS.
10. IT'S ALL IN THE GAME—CLIFF RICHARDS   EPIC
11. QUICKSAND—MARTHA & VANDELLAS   GORDY
12. WHISPERING—APRIL STEVENS & NINO TEMPLE   ATCO
13. AS USUAL—BRENDA LEE   DECCA
14. When You Walk In The Room—Jackie DeShannon   Liberty
15. Got To Dance To Keep From Crying—Miracles   Tamla
16. Louie, Louie—Kingsmen   Wand
17. What Kind of Fool—The Tams   ABC Paramount
18. 442 Glenwood Avenue—Pixies Three   Mercury
19. When the Lovelight—Supremes   Motown
20. Doo-Wah-Diddy—The Exiters   United Artists
21. Send You Back To Georgia—Timmy Shaw   Wand
22. Go and Have Yourself A Ball—Mar-Vells   Butane
23. Um, Um, Um, Um, Um—Major Lance   Okeh
24. Snap Your Fingers—Barbara Lewis   Atlantic
25. Bon Doo Wah—Orlons   Cameo
26. Drag City—Jan & Dean   Liberty
27. Somewhere—Tymes   Parkway
28. Too Bad For You—Sunny Gale   Con-Am
29. Baby, I Love You—Ronettes   Philles
30. Gotta Find A Way—Theresa Lindsey   Correct-Tone
31. Deep In The Heart of Harlem—Clyde McPhatter   Mercury

KEY SONG OF THE WEEK

CALIFORNIA SUN—THE RIVIERAS   RIVIERA

were doing on these shows as not the way we danced, what else were we going to watch? *Soul Train* with Don Cornelius had not been created yet.

We lived on the west side of Detroit within four blocks of the famous Motown recording studio, so I had the opportunity to see a lot of the Motown stars: Temptations, Four Tops, Supremes, Stevie Wonder. We had a chance to see these individuals as they were coming into the Motown Recording Studio. That was a great big thrill for us.

I actually remember playing basketball with one of the Temptations, Melvin Franklin! Melvin Franklin had the deep voice; he was one of the originals. But I grew up with his younger sisters and younger brothers. He liked playing basketball. He wasn't really a good basketball player, but he liked to come on the playground, and of course since I had developed into a key player, everyone would say, "Hey, this guy Marsh is pretty good."

Melvin Franklin was there one day, and, of course, he wanted to play with the best player on the playground that day who was me. I remember him playing and having a great time, and we won several games, and he was very emotional and excited. He was always that kind of individual. I am sure that's what carried him over into the music industry.

Anyway, I remember that after we got through playing, he said, "Come on young fella, I'm going to take you for a ride."

I said, "Ride where?"

He said, "We're fixin to go for a ride in this Cadillac I got."

"Cadillac, man, I ain't never rode in a Cadillac before."

"Yeah, come on young fella, I'm going to take you for a ride in my Cadillac."

So we did; we rode up and down the main strip in our neighborhood. I was grinning from ear to ear. I was riding in a car with Melvin Franklin! So as a kid of thirteen, can you imagine? He put his arm around me and said come for a ride in my Cadillac. Man, that was a moment that I will never forget.

Still, I had to let him know that he was not a basketball player. "Melvin, you are a great, great artist and singer, but basketball? Just leave that alone." But he enjoyed playing and would come out to the playground whenever he was in town and at home.

I was also not related to, but knew, other entertainers from Motown like Smokey Robinson of the Miracles. Smokey had cousins that went to Northern High School. Smokey also attended the Detroit Public Schools.

Just as a side note, I remember just hanging out around some of those Motown celebrities' homes in the hope of being "discovered." As I look back on this whim of mine, I can only laugh at myself wondering "discovered to do what?" I told you earlier that I could not sing.

Again because I was a basketball star, Smokey Robinson wanted to know me, and of course I wanted to know him. His cousins would tell him about me, and he would come to some of our high school basketball games. I got a chance to meet him and be around him. And again, these individuals were larger than life. Motown was larger than life.

I also saw some of the sad parts of Motown when individuals passed away. One member of the Temptations, Paul Williams, who passed away had his funeral at a church in my neighborhood, three or four blocks from where I lived, the Tri-Star Baptist Church.

Back to the 1960s – oh man, what a time to be around, to grow up in. I can't speak for anyone else; I can't speak for my good friend Tommy Daniels, but the 60s was like I was a superstar.

It was a time when I didn't worry about nothing except for basketball and how I could progress in that sport. I started to watch it on TV seeing college players and becoming a student of the game, an historian of the game. I started learning about all those great players who came along prior to the 60s and during the 60s such as John Havlichek of the Boston Celtics and Oscar Robertson of the Cincinnati Royals who later played with the Milwaukee Bucks and who was averaging a triple double before the idea of a triple double even was thought about in the game of basketball: double figures in points, rebounds, and assists. He was a guy who was already doing it.

The 60s was a time where I could watch and learn from the greats in order to become better at basketball. Here again, it did not matter about black or white, only if they were good.

In 1963, I started Hutchins Junior High School. Hutchins was one of the well known middle schools around the city of Detroit, and believe me it wasn't well-known because of its educational standards, but need I say more.

Spider Daniels, who wrote the Foreword of this book, spent 33 years in a middle school in Detroit. He could tell you how it was from a teacher's viewpoint. But again, it was the hand that we were dealt, and we made the best of it. We had great teachers there who were dedicated to working with the kind of students that were coming from these inner-city, low socio-economic families. And again, that is just another way of saying, poor, but I did not know what poor was; I never knew I was poor until somebody told me even though we walked around with holes in our shoes.

My brother showed me how to keep the water from getting to our socks and feet with a technique he developed. He took some plastic wrap and wrapped up cardboard. Now, the hole in the sole was covered and no moisture could get to my socks or feet.

I knew that we were not the only ones walking around with holes in our shoes but at least our feet were dry. But again, no problem, these were still good times. I went through Hutchins Middle School from 1963 to 1966, and also at the same time I was a member of the Boys Club.

Now I know that I mentioned this somewhat before, but I want to emphasize just how huge the Boys Club was to my development. This was a huge, huge thing for me to be involved in because it helped us become better young people by being mentored by adults who provided some structured activities under adult supervision and gave a sense of being a part of an extended family because if you were a "BCer", which stands for a Boys Club member, then you had it going on, and nobody would mess with you if you were a "BCer."

We had arts and crafts, a library, and a gym. There was a variety of activities for all of us depending on or interests. You could get involved at an early age and develop those skills for the interests that you had. My interest, of course, was basketball. So, again I had this opportunity to develop my skills early on because I was participating in structured basketball.

It wasn't a situation where you just threw a ball out like they do nowadays, and everybody starts trying to dribble and shoot and not knowing any skills that you need to start attaining to become a better player. We were taught fundamentals at the Boys Club.

We were taught about hygiene at the Boys Club because if you went up in the gym, I don't care how long you stayed or what you did, when you came back down, you had to take a shower. That taught us right there that when you play, you showered. Now, if you didn't want to shower, then you didn't go up in the gym, but nobody had a problem with showering because when it was your gym time, you wanted to take advantage of that; you didn't want to miss not being able to go to the gym.

I learned how to play basketball to the rhythm of the Motown music.

I learned early on that basketball is a game of rhythm, and rhythm is what can separate you from being an average kind of ball player to being an exceptional ball player. All the great ball players that I ever watched, they looked like ballet artists. You see them flying through the air making different moves, but all to this beat, this rhythm. Long before Air Jordan, all great players including me were set apart by having this rhythm. I wasn't the greatest dancer, but I did have a certain rhythm on that basketball court.

I remember coming into high school in the 60s. I was always playing against guys that were older than I, at least four years older than I was. That is also what contributed to me being the kind of player that I became. There were guys who were high school All-Americans, and I was just coming into high school, thirteen or fourteen years old. Can you imagine? I was pitted against these guys, but again competition makes you better. Bill Talley, high school All-American as a tenth grader; Arnold Stafford, one of the greatest players to ever play at my high school: these guys all paved the way for me.

I remember some crazy incidents in high school. One of the guys who was on the team, probably a second stringer, stole some basketball socks. Of course I was very close with the coach. I was his star player; he had recruited me from the Boys Club and out of junior high school. But anyway, this particular guy stole these basketball socks out of the equipment room where we were working during this work-study program where we could earn a little money. During school you worked in certain areas, and they paid you a small stipend for it. He decided to steal these socks, and I told him, "Listen, I am not going to be a part of this, and I am not going to tell on you either." Back in those days you just were not going to be a snitch no matter what went on. You just didn't snitch. He stole the socks and stupidly came to practice with them in his hand.

Our coach had a way of watching us come into the practice. He would stand up on the balcony track; we were down below. Many of the gymnasiums back in those days had a short running track circling above the basketball court. Coach saw this player coming in with these socks. He called out his name, "Hey!" When the player heard this, he ran downstairs into the locker room. Now mind you, this is high school, so the coach went down there after him and questioned him about where he had gotten those socks. Now, this player knew that coach and I had a tight relationship, so in order to escape he hid the socks and looked over at me and decided to say, "Well, I got them from Cookie." So much for not snitching, but this was an outright lie to cover his ass. I immediately said, "Hell no, you didn't. I am not a part of that."

The coach got frustrated and told the rest of the players, "All right, listen you guys, y'all handle this." The coach went upstairs. We are all downstairs in the locker room, and I am trying to convince this guy, "Go on and give them socks up. We know you got 'em; we saw you walking in here with them." But he wouldn't do it. Some guys on my team were ruthless guys, perhaps you could call them thugs. They found a rope.

"What are you going to do with that rope."

They said, "We are fixin' to hang that sonofabitch; he stole."

"Come on, man, you can't do that."

"Yep, we fixin' to hang him."

My first thought was where in the world did they get a rope in the locker room. Then, they actually made a noose, and I'm trying to convince this guy. He was turning white as a ghost, and he was normally as black as my shoe. He was scared to death knowing they were fixin' to hang him if he did not come up with those socks. When he saw that they were serious, he finally told them where the socks were, and we retrieved the socks and got 'em back to the coach.

The coach considered it over with, but I wonder what would have happened had he not given those socks up. I mean, would we really have been a part of a lynching? But that's just one of the incidents that happened when playing in the PSL (Public School League) and growing up in the environment that we grew up in.

I remember in the 60s going to the Motown Revue. I tell you, you wouldn't miss the Motown Revue because you had a chance to see every artist from the Temptations to the Supremes to the Four Tops to Martha Reeves and the Vandellas to Stevie Wonder. They were all at the Fox Theater in downtown Detroit right around Christmas time. And you did NOT miss that.

I remember going to the Fox Theater one time when I had an abscess tooth; I had a fever, but I sneaked out of the house. It was the most miserable time I ever had because I was sick and sweating, and I couldn't enjoy the show. I was with my brother and sisters who were upset because they had to look after me, but I wanted to see that show so bad, so very bad.

There was another time when we had the opportunity to play basketball at Cobo Arena. Cobo was the place where the Detroit Pistons played their games at that time. Being a part of the Boys Club, we had the opportunity to play another Boys Club team at halftime at Cobo Arena. Again, I am sick, running a fever, strep throat. Again, my Momma told me I better not leave the house, but when she left, I left. I remember going and getting on the bus to ride down there to Cobo, shaking and shivering with a fever. But I just had to do this.

It was a once in a lifetime opportunity to play on the same court that Wilt Chamberlain played on that Oscar Robertson played on, that all the guys on the Detroit Pistons played on. I couldn't miss it; I had to go. So I did. I couldn't even play right. The ball didn't feel right. I think that the fever just took me out of my rhythm. I don't even think I made a shot, maybe a layup. But I just couldn't pass that up. I know I shouldn't have done it. I got in big trouble when I got back home. They went a little light on me, however, because I was sick, but I still got my butt whupped.

We had an opportunity to play for the City Championship. Now, very few high school student-athletes get an opportunity to do this in their high school career. This was 1969 with Detroit Northern vs. Detroit Mumford High School. By the way, our good friend Derek Palm attended Mumford at that time. Although he was not on the team, he was one of the thousands of fans who attended. We had already won our semi-final game against Murray-Wright. Mumford had defeated Northeastern in theirs. This championship game was on a Saturday. That day always sticks in my mind because I knew that it was always around Valentine's Day.

At any rate, we had a full house, probably around nine thousand fans at that game, a high school game. It was a big thrill because that year we got to be celebrities in high school. On Fridays when we had games, we didn't have to go to class. Coach would let us go to the movies. All the teachers would cater to us and excuse us from class. The basketball players were allowed to lounge around, trying to stay off our feet as much as we could because we had to play our game at 3:30.

This wasn't like the Catholic League and other suburban leagues which played their games at night. But there was no way in hell that during the 60s you could have had a Detroit public school game at night. They had tried that; it didn't work; fights broke out with some individuals getting seriously hurt, so the games were moved up to 3:30 with plenty of daylight left. They didn't want to run the chance of violence. But anyway, we ended up losing to Mumford in the City Championship game.

It was an event that will always stand out in my mind. There are still people in 2016 that are blessed to be alive who tell me that they were at that game and remembered me playing.

Even though we lost the game, I was named the MVP for the tournament averaging over thirty points per game. I remember one of the incidents down there at the game at Cobo when one of our fans from Northern set a Mumford girl's hair on fire. She lost a lot of her hair and got burnt. It was ironic that as I went on to college years later, I met that young lady as we both became social workers. When I met her, she said you don't know me, but I was at the game in 1969, and I'm the one whose hair got set on fire. And immediately I could identify with that.

She was now okay, and her hair had grown back and everything, but it was ironic that I would run into her again in my life. It was a sad time that we lost the City Championship, but it was a great time overall.

One thing you have to remember is that out of all the PSL schools, we were some of the sharpest dressers around for high school students. We had guys who wore alligator shoes, snakeskin, lizards, and gabardine shirts.

We were a fashion conscious set of young people, so when we played down at Cobo Arena, as we got ready to go in the locker room, ah man, when we got up, I remember all the people in the stands rise up and watch us go into the locker room because we were super sharp. And all you can hear them saying and whispering is, "Man, look at them boys from Northern; them boys know they're sharp." We prided ourselves on that. I wish we could have won that game because you don't get a second chance to win a City Championship. The experience of the whole thing was so great.

Unfortunately, all was not so great in the late 1960s: the Riots of 1967. Even today, what most people thought was a race riot was definitely not. Being about fifteen years old at the time, I really didn't understand why. Why were people looting, burning and doing this in our own neighborhood?

After the riot was over, we were left with a neighborhood that we had burned down. It wasn't white folks that had burned it down; it was black people. But as I look back on it, it was a very traumatic experience to see an armored tank actually roll down my street, a tank which I had never seen before except on TV and in the movies.

Actually seeing it live was an eye opening experience that I will never ever, ever forget. The size of an Army tank when seeing it coming toward me as a kid and having the Army Reserve enforcing martial law where I lived was something unforgettable.

Furthermore, I remember having some relatives from Mississippi who had come to visit us that summer, and they along with my grandmother, experienced the '67 Riots. They arrived in Detroit just before the Riots. What bad timing for a group who had never been out of Mississippi before. They could not leave and turn around and go back because there were no busses or any transportation leaving out of the city. They would not allow anyone to come into the city either. They were stuck staying with us and enduring three to four days of the Riot before being allowed to leave out of Detroit.

That experience was something they never could have dreamed of. They had heard about the big city and the big lights, automobile plants and all the other things that went on. When you are raised in a rural area in Mississippi, you hear about what goes on in a big city, but they did not anticipate anything like this. Consequently, we all had to sleep on the basement floor hearing gunfire from snipers during the night. My mother would put blankets over us. Then, of course, the relatives couldn't go anywhere to see any sights of Detroit like Belle Isle. Belle Isle is a jewel of the city of Detroit located in the Detroit River between the United States and Canada.

As a side note, a great trivia question is what direction do you have to go from Detroit in order to go to Canada? The answer is surprisingly, south.

Belle Isle was a wonderful place containing an aquarium, a flower house and gardens, a huge marble fountain and a building called a casino. It was not a gambling place that we think of today, but it was a beautiful building where weddings and other receptions took place.

But for the most part, Belle Isle was a place for picnics. It was a place where black and white people could gather for family reunions or just small getaways from the cement and asphalt of the city. New York has Central Park; Rome as Borghese Park; Detroit has Belle Isle. The place became almost a vacation spot, though you could not stay overnight, with its picnic tables, shelters, and, of course, the beach. Whites would not be able to drain the Detroit River after we swam in it.

During the Riots, Belle Isle was turned into a makeshift prison. Because of jail overcrowding, law enforcement would take people out there and lock them up. Of course they couldn't escape because the only exit would be the bridge. No one was going to try to swim the Detroit River that is notorious for a terrible current.

Now think about this situation. My grandmother was born and raised in Mississippi and not used to the commotion of a big city. What would need to happen for this poor lady to really think that the world was coming to an end? Well, before getting into that, let me tell you a little more about her in order to set up what follows. Grandmother was born into times after slavery, living in rural Mississippi until she came up here years later to live after my grandfather died.

Back in Mississippi, no one had a phone except for one relative who had a barber shop in his house. This was more or less a pay phone that people who lived in Blue Ridge, Mississippi would rely on to contact relatives throughout the country. We would phone these relatives John and Liz Bridges leaving a message that we would call back at a certain time. They would go and get my grandparents to make sure they would be at the phone at the designated time.

The point of this aside is that my grandmother never had a phone and never made a phone call in her entire life. In Detroit, my grandmother was terrified to begin with not even wanting to walk the one block to the corner store. She just did not want to deal with it. Then, in 1967 the Riots occurred.

On that very day in July, the rest of our family went to my father's annual work picnic in Walled Lake. Walled Lake was a huge amusement park and picnic grounds located in Walled Lake, Michigan which was a far northwest suburb of Detroit. In those days, going to Walled Lake was a journey. Expressways out that way had not been built yet. Mind you, people back in the 50s and 60s were not as mobile as people are today.

Tom Daniels told me the story about his Aunt Helen who was the only owner and driver of a car in the immediate Daniels' family. She had to stop once or twice for a cigarette break on her way to Sugden Lake for their one week rental of a cottage which was near Walled Lake with the entire distance being about thirty-five miles. Back to that day of our picnic, well, my Grandmother did not want to go. What a mistake in retrospect!

Now remember, our home was at Clairmont and Lee Place which would be considered the New Center area today near Herman Kiefer Hospital right off Twelfth Street where the Riots started. My grandmother, and important to again emphasize here, who had never used a telephone, somehow, some way got the strength and knowledge to contact Walled Lake Amusement Park by phone.

This terrified, old woman with police sirens, gun shots, fires burning, and screaming in the background, miraculously let us know that "the world was coming to an end and that we needed to get home immediately." That must have been a horrific scene for anyone to have described it that way. I have never since heard anyone describe it that way. Poor grandma!

Also, it's odd when you think about prejudice and racism from the viewpoint of a kid and then as an adult.

I remember we would travel every summer. My dad would pack the car, and my mom would fix the lunch which she had to do because we couldn't stop at restaurants once we crossed into Cincinnati. I remember one trip in particular when the car's alternator went out just as we crossed Cincinnati. My dad actually had to drive that car from Cincinnati all the way close to Birmingham, Alabama not because we didn't have the money to get the car fixed but everywhere we stopped at that time were White establishments. They would say things like we don't have the tools or our mechanic just went home or that's a car we don't know how to fix.

Dad knew the real story, but I actually thought it was true that they didn't have the tools and the mechanic had gone home. My daddy was driving a 1961 Chevy Impala, so maybe it was a car they did not know how to fix. But my dad and mom knew what was going on. Dad got in the car, and we drove all the way to Mississippi, and when we stopped for gas, he could not shut off the motor or it would not start up again. This happened just because we were black.

Another traumatic experience was the assassination of Martin Luther King,Jr. in Memphis, Tennessee on April 4, 1968.

I vividly remember that time as I was in high school at Detroit Northern. Teachers and students were all crying just wondering how this man of peace who spearheaded a non-violent protest could have been killed. To me, it stirred an awakening to the possibility that if King could be killed, how safe were the rest of us? Now in relationship to the assassination of President John F. Kennedy which took place five years earlier, because I was in sixth grade then, I really was not too affected. The only serious concern that I had back in junior high was the Cuban Missile Crisis. I remember having to practice hiding under our desks in case there would be an attack. That scared me.

Thomas "Whitey" Daniels | white

University of Detroit High School – what in the world? Understanding that I came from an inner-city, tiny Catholic grade school and ended up at a huge, prestigious high school was bewildering to say the least. The only person I knew in the entire school of eleven hundred boys was Spider, my brother. On that opening day of school, I had only been to the U of D High once before. What had my mother gotten me in to? If it had been up to my father, we both would have attended St. Catherine for high school.

My father had actually attended there before dropping out to go to work. He had very little guidance from his parents growing up due to the fact that he was the second youngest of eleven children. Often, I had wished that dad had gotten his way, but in the long run it was the best decision. Mom was right. Taking two busses from Gratiot and McNichols was a struggle in and of itself,   not so bad on nice days, but in the winter, it was brutal.

Nothing was more welcomed than to see the headlights of the bus coming a half mile away. I remember being on the bus with many black women, who, I learned later on, were going to their maids' jobs in the affluent Palmer Woods and Sherwood Forest area around U of D High. Being a gentleman, I never would keep a seat if one of these ladies was standing even though I had a ton of books and sports equipment. I found myself standing from McNichols and Hamilton (Ponchatrain) to Seven Mile and Cherrylawn.

I had never seen so many students in the same place before! Our eighth grade class at St. Catherine had twenty-five students including the girls. The great equalizer for me, though, was sports. I immediately gained respect by being a starter on the 9th grade football team. I wasn't intimidated by any of the players' skills, but I was amazed at some of their size. I was a 5'9" 130 pounder at the time. I was a tough defensive player, playing both defensive end and linebacker which I played throughout high school except for junior year when I did not go out for the team despite the coach pleading with me to play. Playing football and not playing football were two of the greatest lessons in my life.

High school was tough on me. The homework, the bus rides, the long hours with sports really taught me self-discipline and determination. We could never do any homework at school because all homework had to be in fountain pen, not ball point pen. If you had a fountain pen, you would be in detention. A fountain pen was refillable by liquid ink or a cartridge of liquid ink. Some of you older readers will remember the wooden desks that had a hole cut out on the top called an inkwell to accommodate the bottle of ink. The ball point pen was a relatively new invention in the 1950s. The fountain pen could be very sloppy as you might imagine. Homework was for home! Schoolwork done in pencil or ballpoint pen was for school. Could you imagine enforcing that rule today?

I played two sports in high school: baseball and football. However, it was during high school that my love of basketball and my skills developed. I was a very late starter in the game of basketball. I never played it up until eighth grade.

I tried out for the team in 7th grade and got cut. It probably had something to do with when in layup lines (we called them dog shots back then) I shot the ball into the balcony.

Or it could have been my stylish shorts. I didn't have any shorts let alone basketball shorts. I never wore them as a kid, always jeans. Anyway, faced with the fact that I needed shorts for tryouts, my mother sewed the fly of a pair of my father's polka dotted boxer underwear, and I wore them.

Assumption Grotto Grade School gym with Mr. Hayner, our supervisor, was where I began to improve and began to become addicted to basketball. Mondays and Wednesdays we would be at open gym there, and Tuesdays we would go to Denby High School to play. Saturdays you would see me at Cannon Recreation Center next to what eventually became Finney High School.

Converse Chuck Taylors were the shoes of choice. As a matter of fact, they were the only choice, no Adiddas, no Nikes, no Pumas, only Chucks as they were affectionately called. We couldn't afford the good ones, so I got the ones that had some sort of blemish that cost not the ungodly eleven dollars but around six dollars. I didn't care; I was styling in my Chucks.

I eventually improved in basketball playing in recreation leagues and intra-murals at U of D High. I got better and might have made the school team, but we were loaded in those years even beating Rudy Tomjanovich and his Hamtramck team in a district title game. Our star players included Andy Szombati who went on to play on the University of Detroit Freshman Team, Bill Thigpen, Ed Petersmark, Mark Bonczak, Tim Cooney, Pat Davis, and Tom Eckert. I became a selected all-star in the intra-mural league winning the junior class championship. There will be more about basketball as I tell about college and later years.

At U of D High I had a mixture of friends. Earlier Cookie talked about shared experiences making people grow closer. Bill Thigpen, may God rest his soul, shared the bus with me. Bill, a black guy, was a giant for those days, 6'5." He was another who came from a distance to U of D High. I wonder what he really was thinking about that whole experience as well. He was a terrific basketball player, and he along with Ed Petersmark (6'6") formed a monstrous front line for those days at least.

I had many acquaintances from high school, but because of the distance that I lived from school and never having a car, they were only school friends. I was there to get an education and play sports.

For some people, high school, if not the best time of their lives, was at least a great time. Although highly impressionable, for me, they were difficult times. I will never forget when in geometry class we heard the news of the assassination of President John F. Kennedy. It was Friday around 2:00 p.m. Coincidentally, it was the same day of the Goodfellows Football Game down at Tiger Stadium between the Catholic League Champion and the Public School Champion. The game was played. I was there. I guess life must go on. I will never forget the fear I had of the Cuban Missile Crisis. One afternoon, I was preparing to go out to football practice, and I was thinking, what for? Why go through this grueling practice when the world was going to end anyway? Good thing I went to practice; we are still here.

Baseball was very, very good to me. As a sophomore, I made the varsity and ended up starting due to an illness/injury to the senior who was the starting second baseman. I made the most of my opportunity as we won the league after a playoff between four teams: Catholic Central, Notre Dame, Austin, and us who had tied for the title. I averaged .346 for the season. We had a terrible game in the Catholic League semi-final over at Butzel Park at Lyndon and Myers. Had we won, we would have played for the Catholic League title at Tiger Stadium. I made all-league as a junior, batting .364 in a tough league loaded with college bound pitchers, and was captain as a senior.

Our team struggled those years, but I played well and kept getting better by playing in the summer time. I must honor Larry Weis, a tremendous youth league supporter and coach who took me under his wing during my formative years. He taught me the intricacies of the game through meetings in the off-season and statistics.

Also, I must mention Joe Bialk whose younger brother Tom was on the team. Joe was our assistant coach, and after his work at the factory, he would load us up in his car and take us to the games. With sometimes eight or nine of us piled into the car, who used seat belts? Were they even in every car back then? Joe was a great baseball player in his own right and being a second baseman taught me a lot. Playing on teams like A&B Brokers and Harper Sports Shop, we played four times per week.

Coach Weis gave me the opportunity to play in Tiger Stadium twice. Unforgettable! In fact, I hit one into the seats at Tiger Stadium. Swinging late on a fastball, I fouled it into the seats near third base. Now, how many people can say they hit one into the seats at Tiger Stadium?

My biggest disappointment was being cut from the Kowalski team which had dominated the national tournaments for years. To this day I cannot figure that one out. I tried out for the team and did well. I was certainly better than the other second baseman but found myself being tried out at shortstop – not my natural position. I think it had something to do with politics which I did not understand at that time. Ted Simmons of the St. Louis Cardinals had played for Kowalski before I tried out.

TIGER STADIUM

I found myself one year on the Bruins coached by a fine black man by the name of Gene Holmes. Prior to that, the only all black opponents were the West Side Cubs and New Bethel. Coincidentally, many years later, Ron Teasley who had been a West Side Cub became one of our geezers. Ron was a transplant from the West Side to play baseball at Denby High on the far East Side of Detroit. That season with the Bruins was a lot of fun. Again, as Cookie said, it didn't matter if you were black or white but if you could play the game.

I had a couple of blind dates in high school, didn't go to my prom, although I could have with a baseball friend's sister. But I had no money and no car so going would have been a hardship. I was very shy anyway. So, that night of the prom I probably stayed home and watched sports on television.

There is a humorous story about the guy who was buying train tickets and encountered the ticket seller who was a well endowed woman with lots of cleavage. When it was his turn to request his tickets, all he could say was, "Could I have two pickets to Tittsburgh." That guy would have been me for sure.

At U of D High, we had sock hops and hootenannies to mix with the girls from Immaculata High School, an all-girls school near Marygrove College off of McNichols (Six Mile). I went to some of these events, really never talked to a girl there.

We had Monday night teen club dances at Assumption Grotto for high school students. The guys would be on one side of the hall talking football, etc. It was a good time to meet guys from other high schools like Harper Woods Notre Dame and DeLaSalle that we would play in football and other sports. There were absolutely no black boys or girls there.

Sometimes I would dance a slow dance. I remember one time the DJ called out "Ladies' Choice." I thought that a lady had chosen that particular song to be played, so I gathered up my nerve to ask a girl to dance with me. Later on, I realized that "Ladies' Choice" meant the girls could choose whom they wanted to dance with. Oh boy!

Another call by the DJ was "Snowball." No, I did not go outside to pack one. I realized that it meant to change partners until everyone was up and dancing. Those were probably the times when I was asked to dance.

Within sports, I learned some major lessons. The first one was that sometimes things just aren't fair. Okay, so you have to go on and make the best of what remains. Not making the Kowalski team really threw me for a loop. Confidence damaged, it was too late to hook on with another team for that summer. Coach Weis had stopped coaching. I was lost. To this day, I wonder if that one lost season set me back irrevocably. Especially in baseball where developing the ability to hit ever increasingly difficult pitching, missing a year of this progression was critical.

Another lesson was learned when I did not play football as a junior but re-joined the team as a senior. Second guessing myself for not playing was not an option. I really did not like football. Every year in his opening remarks, the coach of each team would say, "If you don't love contact, go home right now!" I always wondered if we were really honest with ourselves, how many would have remained on the team. Now, it wasn't that I was a wimp. As a matter of fact, Coach Frank Buford at our high school football banquet praised me as one of the toughest kids he had coached. On the field, I backed down to no one. I didn't like it, but I was too scared to fail.

Back to the lesson learned. I killed myself to become the starting defensive end on the varsity my senior year. At 5'10" and 155 pounds, I was, to say the least, undersized. We had a night time scrimmage to begin the season at Ferndale High School under the lights. I should have been excited; I was exhausted. When I got home after school that Friday, all I wanted to do was sleep. I was beaten to shit by the three a day practices which we had just endured in the blistering heat of   August, 1965.

Back in those days, coaches did not know any better, limiting our water intake and offering us salt pills from the dispenser by the locker room exit. Can you imagine that being the case today? I had earned my starting position, but at what cost? I got murdered at the scrimmage, and the coaches noticed. It took me almost all season to regain some playing time. I did not quit; I practiced hard; I learned to persevere despite a major setback. I also realized that I only had myself to blame because I was the one who did not play junior year. Consequences for actions.

What can be said about the music of the 60s? While my parents were listening to the Big Band sounds of the 1940s as well as some intermittent classicals and instrumentals, I was into the music explosion of rock-n-roll, the Beatles, Rolling Stones and, of course,

Motown! What an incredible era to have grown up in as far as music was concerned!

Probably my first recollection of songs were "The Lion Sleeps Tonight" (can anyone say awimbawack, awimbawack?) and Roy Orbison's "Crying over You." The Rolling Stones' "This Could Be the Last Time" and "Time Is on My Side" blared in our football locker room as we either prepared to go out for the dreaded practice or returned licking our wounds to shower and go home. But nothing- and I mean nothing- could top the Motown Sound.

I was in love with the Temptations. My brother and I would wear out the rug doing the Temptation Walk in our living room at 18052 Pelkey(by the way, we also lived at 18054 Pelkey, not a horizontal move but a vertical move to the lower flat from the upper flat). We also wore out the 331/3 LPs that we listened to each and every chance we had. High on my list for a Christmas gift was always a Motown album. The Miracles were a distant second to David, Eddie, Paul, Otis, and Melvin. They kept me company on those angry Friday evenings when I had to stay home to babysit my little sister Mary when I wanted to be at a high school football or basketball game.

My mom had gone back to work at Sears and Roebuck at Gratiot and Van Dyke when Bob and I entered high school probably to pay for our exorbitant tuition which was a whopping $260 per year when we started at U of D High.

My parents tolerated this music with only the occasional, "Why are you listening to that Jungle Bunny music (whatever that meant) or "I can't understand one word they are singing" or "all that music sounds the same." I really believe that music and sports were the catalysts to integration. I did not care if the singer was black or white. I did not care if the player was black or white. As long as he/she could perform was all that mattered.

Do you remember a group that came along in the 70s called AWB (Average White Band)? Well, one of their hits was "Play That Funky Music, White Boy." Blacks and whites alike love that tune. Whether it was the Drifters or the Four Tops or Martha Reeves and the Vandellas or the Kinks, Bob Seger, or the Monkees, it did not matter. Toleration, respect and acceptance were learned through music and sports. Probably the best memory was seeing the Temptations live at the Michigan State Fair.

I had mentioned that I did not play football my junior year. Part of the reason was that I had my first part time job working at Baskin-Robbins 31 Flavors on McNichols near Gunston. I was a terrible worker: nervous, unskilled, and just awful. My training was sketchy at best.

Anyway, there was another Tom who worked there. I wanted to go to the State Fair with Spider and Joe Nowaske that Sunday. Probably through the eyes of wishful thinking, I read the work schedule wrong and missed work that Sunday. I was subsequently fired from my first job. The manager called my mother as we were at the State Fair. Oh boy, I had some explaining to do when I got home after that euphoric experience with the Temptations. Oh well, seeing the Temptations was well worth it.

The three of us hitch hiked from Schoenherr and McNichols to Woodward and Eight Mile. The concert area was packed when we got there. Spider (monkey) ended up in a tree to watch the show. Somehow, Joe and I got up on the roof of a nearby building and had a great view as Tammi Terrell came out in a very tight, sequined dress as the crowd went crazy. When the Temptations came out, the integrated crowd went berserk!

One of my regrets from this time frame was that I never went to the Motown Review at the Fox Theater. I really do not remember why I never went. It possibly had to do with the perception that it was a black thing. I know that Cookie was there, and I am jealous of him for that.

Just a few months ago I came across a WKNR music chart from December 26, 1963. WKNR along with CKLW and WXYZ were pop music stations back then. Disc Jockeys like Lee Allen on the horn and Robin Seymour of *Swingin' Time* and Gary Stevens played music from black and white artists. As a matter of fact, the music of this time crossed the parallel lines into blacks listening to white artists and whites enjoying black artists.

Both black teenagers and whites deserve credit for their courageous actions in the face of their parents' disapproval if not anger for their listening to "that" music. Some covers of black artists' albums did not depict the black singer to hide what the white kids were buying from their parents. This prejudicial thinking did not deter the teenagers of this era. Regardless, on this same hit chart were Roy Orbison, Bobby Rydell, and Bobby Vee sharing success with the Marvelettes, Martha Reeves and the Vandellas, and the Miracles. Dionne Warwick was at the top with "Anyone Who Had a Heart."

How can you reflect on the 1960s without thinking about the racial tensions of the country? I saw the Marches and Demonstrations on television and certainly sympathized with the blacks and their struggles. I was shocked when I heard on my way to baseball practice at the University of Detroit that Dr. Martin Luther King Jr. was assassinated. I read a book on Malcolm X; I read the book Black Like Me (to which this book's title alludes). I was sensitive to discrimination and segregation. I didn't like it; I thought George Wallace and those other racists were evil.

The Detroit Riots were a fearful time. They affected me in some strange ways. That summer I was working at Sears at the Macomb Mall, Masonic and Gratiot, a long way from Twelfth Street in Detroit. Yet, all the buzz was "Are they coming?" The store manager had every plate glass display window covered with plywood as if a massive hurricane was about to strike. I was nervous.

Spider had gone to a Detroit Tiger game that Sunday of the Riots, taking the bus to and from. When he arrived home, he got the news that the Riots had broken out being oblivious to how close he had been just minutes before. You have to remember that instant communication was not available as it is today, no cell phones especially.

My other recollection was the curfew that was imposed on the citizens of Detroit. My friends and I decided to get out of town and traveled to East Lansing to hang out with fraternity brothers from Michigan State University. We just cleared the Eight Mile border when the curfew went into effect

CHAPTER 4
The College Years

Thomas "Cookie" Marsh | *black*

Yep, and then came the babies! A lot of people might be a little apprehensive or even shamed about what I am going to talk about. I have seven adult children right now and twenty-one grandchildren, one great-grandchild and one on the way.

Now, I got married right out of high school. There were some good sides to that and some down sides. Downside is, I never learned how to cook, and so I am really, really dependent on my loving wife now, my previous wife and whatever girlfriends I had. When you are eighteen years old and you leave from your mama's house, you are used to eating your mama's cooking. When I got married at eighteen, hey, I was eating my wife's cooking. Right then at eighteen years old herself, the main thing she knew how to cook was Hamburger Helper. And I mean I had Hamburger Helper in every shape or form or fashion that you could have it in: Hamburger Helper tuna, Hamburger Helper salami, Hamburger Helper macaroni and cheese, Hamburger Helper chicken.

Anyway, my oldest daughter and my oldest son were born thirty days apart: one was born on April 21st and the other was May 21st. Obviously, they were born by two different women. I am not going to elaborate on that because you can imagine what kind of dilemma that caused.

When I announced this dilemma to my parents, I remember my grandmother yelling from the back room, "Castrate the boy!" My mother replied quite surprisingly, "Shut up!" I did not know what castrate meant at the time. But, all in all with all of my children, I feel blessed because I was a part of all of their lives.

My oldest daughter was by another woman other than my current wife. It took up until she was almost an adult until she was finally told who her biological father was. She was brought up to think that her surrogate dad was actually her biological father. Now, this is something that her mother wanted to happen. This is something that I didn't agree to, and I have to admit that at that age, having a child when you are only about eighteen years old was a very difficult time for me. I was really immature and did not know how to handle the situation. And you have to remember that I am in the midst of my basketball career getting ready to go to college. I really didn't know anything about having a child.

Actually I didn't even think that I could make a baby, but evidently I could. But through the years, everything worked out, and, as I said before, I am blessed to have a relationship with all of my children. I am blessed to have a relationship with all of my grandchildren. It's really a great time when we are all together on Christmas or Thanksgiving and are able to see all of them together. It is a feeling that I just can not explain.

Now I remember back in high school feeling like those were the best times of my life. A lot of people say that college was their best time, but for me it was definitely high school. The only things I was concerned with was what I was going to wear to school or if I was fitting in with my peers and playing basketball which gave me celebrity status. But over the years, the greatest thing about basketball for me was the fact that it enabled me to get a college degree.

I know a lot of young people who went down the same path that I did in terms of being a high school All-American thinking that I would be the next Michael Jordan or Isiah Thomas. But the truth of the matter is that only one out of thousands/millions reach that status. I am extremely proud that I finally graduated even though it was thirteen years after I was supposed to graduate from the University of Detroit in 1973. I went back and finished my degree.

THOMAS "COOKIE" MARSH

Here, I must mention a very influential professor of mine at U of D Mrs. Angela Kennedy. She recognized that I was not the traditional college student, but one who was struggling through a divorce and trying to get my degree after a long layoff. She was wonderful. I credit her with getting my degree as well as getting my head together.

She was the wife of Harry Kennedy who mentored me at the Boys Club. What a special couple who, as I said before, I now call neighbors. The University of Detroit was very good to me not charging a dime for this completion. The degree opened up a lot of doors in terms of employment for me. It completed a task that we as black families have always instilled in our young to complete your education, to better yourself, your family and your community.

I was the first in my entire family to get a college degree; Tom was the second in his family as his older brother Spider beat him by a year. How blessed was I? A full sixteen credit load in 1968 was $638. Today, you would get one single credit for that. Can you imagine the difference in tuition thirteen years later when I returned?

On my first shift as a college student, I only cared about getting by so that I could remain eligible to play college basketball. What did I care? I was going to the NBA.

I always knew I could get good grades, but everything in my life had been pointing to an NBA career. I didn't apply myself to school. But I didn't have an NBA career.

I go back to college thirteen years later and actually become serious about my education. I was a 4.0 student which I probably could have been in the first place. It was about applying myself and getting my priorities straight.

I hope young people who read this story truly read this section. And when they get an educational chance, they will understand that it is all about doing the best and being the best that they can. Don't just be "eligible." You want to be the best student that you can be. If you can be an "A" student, be an "A" student. If your potential is to be a 2.5 student, be that. But don't ever sell yourself short and say I am just going to get the minimum requirement because it will certainly come back to haunt you.

I remember my experience when it was time to go to college and choosing a university. I had many offers for basketball scholarships. But academically, I wasn't ready. I carried a 2.5 in high school which was not even in core subjects and scored low on the SAT.

Despite many poor choices and mistakes, God was watching over me. Everything that happened was for a purpose. I am a better man, husband, social worker, father, grandfather, great grandfather because of these trials and tribulations. I am able to advise young people so much better. They say whatever difficulties you have make you stronger as long as they didn't kill you. I didn't get killed nor did I get castrated. Obviously!

Thomas "Whitey" Daniels | white

Upon graduating from U of D High School, I immediately enrolled at the University of Detroit, again following my brother's footsteps. Truly, I did not even think about it. It felt like I was going to thirteenth grade except at a school that was one mile south and one mile east. U of D was basically an all-white college when I enrolled.

I credit the Viet Nam War and my mother for my college degree. My mother expected me to go to college and graduate in four years. Spider became the first Daniels to ever graduate from college, and I was the second. As proof that this accomplishment was just an expectation and not a remarkable achievement, neither of my parents attended the graduation ceremony for either my brother or me. We have few if any pictures, videos, cards, etc. Why should we? Expectations. Had I not graduated, I probably would have been killed in the Viet Nam War or by my mother.

Speaking of that War, I had the good fortune to have been selected number 315 in the draft lottery that was determined by the order that your birthday was selected in the lottery. The United States instituted the Selective Service Act which would force young men into the military. It was called subscription, not to a magazine but to a war. As I recall, only the unfortunate numbers up to approximately thirty-five caused induction into the armed forces.

Spider was less fortunate. His birthday came up as number 28. I remember the fear on my mother's face when she and I saw that selection on television. Spider wasn't home at the time, probably a good thing. My mother may have sent him to Canada to avoid having to go. Spider went down for the dreaded physical at Ft. Wayne in Detroit. Timing was great for him as he had just graduated from college and became a teacher which gave him an exempt status. Whew!!

I noticed that the Selective Service System really was selective. Boys from poor neighborhoods and blacks seemed to be "selected" at a far greater rate than the rich boys who could get college exemptions and who had connections that helped them to be accepted into the Reserves and avoid Viet Nam. It was a common practice for draftees to cross the border, going south into Canada knowing that they may never return to their homes in the United States again. How sad this was for them and their families.

During that time, Cassius Clay became Muhammad Ali and claimed to be a conscientious objector and refused to be drafted into the United States Armed Forces. Of course that scenario caused quite an uproar especially when other celebrities and professional athletes had served in the army. Ted Williams was a prime example who served in World War II during the height of his illustrious baseball career.

Thousands of parents had to say goodbye, in many cases permanently, to their sons as they went to Viet Nam or Canada, yet here was the Heavyweight Champion of the World avoiding the draft. Ali, however, was sanctioned, and I do not want to get into that whole thing here. As Forest Gump would say, "That's all I have to say about that."

Many years later, I believe it was President Gerald Ford who granted amnesty, and the exiled returned to their homes in the United States. All kinds of actions were taken to avoid going to the War: shooting/cutting off fingers and toes; taking medications to raise blood pressure to an unacceptable level before the physical exam prior to induction; tremendous weight gain in order to be deemed obese and unfit for duty. Years later I learned, regretfully, that those who were rich were spared.

If you remember, the classic Credence Clearwater Revival song "Fortunate Son," depicted this kind of disparity:

Some folks are born made to wave the flag
Ooh, they're red, white and blue
And when the band plays "Hail to the chief"
Ooh, they point the cannon at you, Lord
It ain't me, it ain't me, I ain't no senator's son, son
It ain't me; it ain't me, I ain't no fortunate one, no

Anyway, enough of the heavy music. My college years were fantastic!! U of D High had given me the structure and discipline to basically make college easy. We had to take classes that were boring such as music appreciation and twelve credit hours in philosophy along with eight credit hours in theology (after all it was a Catholic university). But really, who cared? My social life finally began. I found lifelong friends, alcohol, and a fraternity, Theta XI.

During college, my life became even more segregated. U of D was lily white except for the basketball team. The basketball team had been integrated by the likes of Dorie Murray, Lou Hyatt, and Dwight Dunlap and eventually Spencer Haywood, the Gold Medal winner in the 1968 Olympics. But most players had been white like Dave DeBusschere who starred at Austin High School in the late 50s. Others were Bobby Calihan, Jr., Bruce Rodwan, and Larry Salci. Larry was a terrific basketball player and baseball pitcher. I had the opportunity to play on the same team with him at U. of D. in 1968.

Curiously, we only saw Larry when it was his turn to pitch. I guess Coach Bob Miller had made a deal with Larry that he need not come to practice, just to games that he would pitch. After all, Larry was a senior and had just finished a grueling basketball season. We were all grateful that he even consented to be with us at all. He was very good!

Here I must relate an embarrassing story that involved me and Larry during a U of D baseball game. You know how there are incidents in your life that haunt you, and you wish you could go back and make a change? This is one.

Larry was pitching a terrific game; it was extra innings; he had pitched the entire game. Finally, in the bottom of the tenth inning, we put runners on second and third with one out. Yours truly was at the plate. As a player, you dream of these opportunities. This one turned out to be a nightmare.

Well, I was an excellent bunter, and Coach Miller signaled for the suicide squeeze meaning that the runner on third will run to the plate while I laid down a bunt which would win the game for us and Larry. Seems simple, right? I "overheard" the pitcher and catcher say that they were going to walk me to load the bases and set up the double play. Makes sense, right, with first base open? The pitch was right down the middle, and I stood there as Ernie Harwell would say, "Like the house at the side of the road."

I could have bunted that ball with my eyes closed and won the game. Disaster! Our runner from third was a dead duck at the plate for the second out of the inning. But wait; it gets worse. Our runner on second base is caught in a rundown between second and third facing the third out of the inning.

Coach Miller, rightfully so, threw his hat and cursed. I watched hopelessly until the shortstop threw the ball over the third baseman's head allowing our runner to score. We and Larry won the game. I wonder if Salci and Coach Miller remember that game. I surely hope not.

Reflecting on the city of Detroit and the country at large, the late 60's and early 70's at U of D were a time of change. Bob Calihan had been the basketball coach forever and nearing time for retirement. Unfortunately, the University was not ready for a black basketball coach even though Will Robinson, the legendary high school coach at Pershing, would have been able to put U of D basketball on the map as a Division I powerhouse for eternity.

Coach Robinson would have been able to recruit the fertile grounds of the Detroit Public Schools where Cookie and a large number of other great players attended. Instead, Jim Harding was selected, a strict disciplinarian with no roots in the basketball rich Detroit community. Cookie will be going into further detail here because he lived this transition.

My interest in basketball continued to escalate as Andy Szombati, one of my classmates from U of D High, was on the freshmen team at U of D along with Pat Cahill, a new acquaintance who had starred at Redford St. Mary's and John Parker, a star from Austin High School. Back in those days, freshmen were not allowed to play on the varsity no matter how good they might be.

I also loved going down to Cobo Arena to watch the Detroit Pistons. Who can forget Gus, one of the vendors whose route was up in the "yellows" – the cheap seats in the arena. Those seats could not have cost more than two to three dollars. Can you imagine compared to ticket prices these days? Gus would begin gyrating to a song as Tyrone Hemphill, the organ player-that's right, organ player- would break into a peppy tune. The crowd would go nuts. We loved Gus!

Those days are long gone because of the Piston move to, initially, the Silverdome and then to the Palace of Auburn Hills and soon to be Detroit. Now, who could afford tickets, and how could the regular person get out there? Cookie's father in disgust stated, "Now they have taken the players out to the plantation." "DEE-troit Basketball!" Not really.

Besides being a spectator, it did not take long before I found a Thursday morning group that played basketball at the Memorial Building-now called Calihan Hall. We played religiously at 11:00.

I use the term religiously due to the fact that the entire academic program shut down on Thursdays at 11:00 so that the college community could go to Mass. We, on the other hand, attended the church of St. Chuck Taylor.

It was on one of those Thursday mornings that I noticed Dave Bing, my basketball hero from the Detroit Pistons, shooting down at the other end. Before long a half court three on three game began. I was guarding Dave Bing! He went up for a shot and I snuffed it. He said, "Nice going." How many people do you know can say that they blocked the shot of a Hall of Famer? It was luck, but it was still a memory.

Those Thursday mornings eventually led to a college wide intramural basketball championship. Ray McDonald, Norm Dick, Pat Cahill, Spider, Joe Nowaske and I tore it up.

Joining the Theta Xi fraternity turned out to be one of the best moves I ever made. Going to the "Rush Parties" was a lot of fun. Everyone treated you great, and the beer was free. Spider and I took great advantage of those parties. I never drank alcohol in high school, just never had the means, motive, or opportunity.

My first encounter was on a trip to New York City at the end of our freshmen year in college with Spider, Pat Cahill, and Mark Kronk. We had one of those cheesy fake headlines for a newspaper made that read "Boosh, Spider, Pat and T Boogaloo through NYC." We thought we were the shit! I did not want to see or taste Southern Comfort for a long time after that trip. Ouch!

Then, one Sunday morning after Mass at Assumption Grotto Church, I noticed Spider getting ready to go somewhere. We had never talked about actually joining a fraternity. So, again, following his footsteps, I got ready and went with him to the fraternity meeting where we actually began the process of pledging Theta Xi Fraternity.

What in the world had I gotten myself in to? All that fun and camaraderie turned into a nightmare, or at least for the ten weeks I pledged. As a pledge, I basically became a slave to the existing members. The only thing our pledge class had going was our size- eighteen of us. So there were a lot of us to share the abuse.

Hell Weekend was named only partly correct. It was hell, but "only" lasted from Friday at 5:00p.m. until about the same time on Saturday. Had it lasted any longer, I think some of us would have died, literally. We were basically kidnapped to a farm in Canada about twenty miles from the tunnel. We had been tuned up for about two hours previously by members of the fraternity who selected individual pledges for the torture.

Dressed in heavy clothing and cumbersome boots (the old style with the buckles) due to the cold late November weather, I was put through calisthenics and running. I was grateful to get into the van to be transported to Canada. Was I wrong in thinking things would get better. At the farm, the eighteen of us were re-united. The fraternity members were in a foul mood.

TALENT SHOW CHAMPS

I can only compare what took place to a prison camp that I may have seen in a movie. We began a "death march" that lasted all night and into the next day. To say I was miserable would be putting it mildly. Leg cramps continued from midnight to dawn. Finally they allowed us some rest. Needless to say, I would never do this again.

Happier times began immediately when we found out that at 6:00 p.m. on that Saturday, we were full-fledged members of Theta Xi Fraternity. Being in that fraternity eventually soothed the pain of pledging, and we had great times.

Winning the University of Detroit all fraternity and sorority Talent Show was unforgettable. I had mentioned earlier my love of the Temptations.

Well, we put together a show based on their music complete with a band, a skit to interpret the lyrics and the impersonated singers of whom I was one. When Spider as David Ruffin came out with a twirl and the splits, the crowd went nuts. Dick Heitman had dressed as a woman giving credence to the tune, "Beauty's Only Skin Deep."

This was a great accomplishment; however, I had promised myself that I would study for my mid-term American Lit. exam after the performance. Whom do I think I was kidding? Not even myself. We partied hard that night. I got what I deserved on the exam, an "F."

I have no regrets.

CHAPTER 5

Dream Assassinated

Thomas "Cookie" Marsh | *black*

As I wrote earlier, I was a great player. During high school and college in the summer time, I would play against all the best players including professionals. At that time and even into today, St. Cecila's, a small gymnasium on Livernois on the west side of Detroit now run by Sammy Washington and previously by his father, was the hot bed of basketball. Whites and blacks sweated there together both trying to avoid the support beams that were way too close to the sidelines.

Tom Daniels brought his Royal Oak Kimball team to St. Cecilia to give them a taste of what real basketball was, not just some suburban style. Professionals and college players met there to scrimmage as well as play in leagues.

Heck, they even have created a hall of fame for its great players. My picture is hanging there on the wall. Not only was I a tremendous jump shooter with unlimited range, but also I knew how to play the game. Coach Taylor at Northern and Coach Harding at U of D made sure of that. I learned that basketball is played inside out:

get the ball to the big men inside and let them do their thing or have them pass it back out as the defense collapsed. I learned that I must be able to play on both ends of the floor both offense and defense. Therefore, coming out of college, I was the complete package.

My first disappointment was that I was not drafted by any NBA team out of college. Guys that I knew very well and who were not as good as I was were being drafted right and left.

Okay, I accepted that and attributed my snub to the style of basketball we played at U of D. Coach Harding was a controller. Yes, we won a lot of games, but scoring was low as we played a very patient style of offense. As a result, my scoring average was relatively low, about fourteen points per game. Certainly, no NBA scouts were impressed by a relatively low scoring guard from a college that was not considered an elite program.

Therefore, in order to keep my life long dream of an NBA career alive, I went to the Pistons rookie camp at Eastern Michigan University as a free agent. Remember, in my mind as an immature young person, the NBA was the only career that I had been preparing for. This was it, basically do or die!

At the rookie camp, I was by far the best player. The drafted players were nowhere near my level of play. Coaches took notice that I was a great shooter and a complete player. Basically, I breezed through rookie camp and was one of only three who was asked to return to the veterans' camp the following week. My NBA dream was nearing fulfillment!

And, again, not so fast, Cookie Marsh. Yes, at veterans' camp, I again displayed my total skills. At the time, Bob Lanier and Dave Bing were the stars of the Pistons. Coaches were impressed that I knew the "inside out" theory of the game keeping Lanier happy as he was the man in the middle.

They took notice of how I was able to defend as well. They obviously liked the way I could shoot because I was exceeding even George Trapp who was the Pistons' best outside shooter at the time.

Two days into the veterans' camp, I heard some disturbing rumors. Now realize, a basketball team only has room for a certain amount of guards, and contracts, politics, and public relations come into the formula. In other words, the decision whether to keep a player or not is not solely based on his talent level.

Stu Lantz, an NBA veteran of thirteen years, had previously stated that he was not coming back for his final option year. That week at camp, he changed his mind and was automatically given one of the guard spots. Becoming a little nervous, I still believed that the one remaining spot was mine. I earned it!

Ben Kelso had been the Pistons second round draft pick the year before but opted to stay at EMU for his final season instead of joining the Pistons. Now this year, he was looked upon as the Pistons #1 draft pick. Ben at 6'3" was more of a swing man than a guard, so I thought that I still had the chance for the final guard spot.

Now, mind you, when I say final guard spot, I am not conceding that I was the worst guard in the mix – far from it. I believe that as a rookie, I would be making an impact. Remember, I had played with all of these players very often over the years. I knew where I stood in relation to their talent.

The news of Justice Thigpen, another guard, being released brightened my hopes that I was still in the running to make the team. With these worries heavy on my mind, I went in to talk to Coach Ray Scott. I told him of my concerns. He was very up front and kind to me, BUT . . .

Coach Ray Scott:
"Cookie, you will not make the Detroit Pistons."

Judge Geraldine Ford:
"Thomas Curtis Marsh, thirty days in the
Detroit House of Correction."

Now to fill in the time between these two earth shattering events.

Which was worse? The crashing sound made by the jail door shutting on me for the next thirty days or the crashing sound of Ray Scott's voice closing the door on my lifelong dream?

Shattered, depressed, I found myself working out at Calihan Hall on the campus of the University of Detroit, my home away from home, prior to the team's practice session. I was in a fog and certainly on edge.

A security guard, who always seemed to be on the lookout for me, entered the gym to remove me from the premises stating that I was trespassing. Now, mind you, I had just finished a brilliant career and felt that this was truly my home. I had spent countless hours representing this fine institution on the hardwood. How could I be trespassing in my own backyard?

Well, this petty potentate looked upon the situation quite differently. He had some power, and he was going to use it. "Get out!" With that he grabbed my arm and started to pull me toward the exit.

The rest was a blur and still is. The report states that I continued to strike him until pulled off. I lost all control with the disappointment and anger of the past fueling my fists. The guard pressed charges for assault and trespassing.

To the University's credit, the guard was urged not to go forward with the charges or he would risk losing his job. The guard was fired; I went to jail.

I had never been in trouble with the law; I had no criminal record. How could I be going to jail? My family was in the court room that day after just returning from Mississippi burying my grandmother. We were all prepared to pay a fine and for me to be placed on probation. No dice! Apparently the judge held some sort of grudge against a friend of mine due to her daughter's association with him. She couldn't get back at him, but she surely could get me. "Thirty days!"

Don't Look Back

If you just put your hand in mine.
We're gonna leave all our troubles behind.
We're gonna walk and don't look back.
And don't look back. Oh yeah, yeah.
And don't look back, baby.
The past is behind you let nothing remind you.

"Don't look back!" How many times did I sing along with the Temptations to that song? How could I have ever known that those words would apply to me in a so much different manner? As they say, what doesn't kill you makes you stronger. Twenty hours per day I exercised. What else was there to do? I not only became physically stronger but mentally and emotionally as well.

I resolved then and there and promised God that I would never allow myself to lose control. I resolved to never cross that line again. I have kept that vow.

As I left the Detroit House of Correction (what a name for a jail, huh?), I remembered the words from other convicts who said that if you look back as you are exiting the jail, you will be back. My eyes were focused forward as they have been ever since.

What gives someone the license to lose control? Does anything ever good come out of this lack of regard for consequences? Every day the media reports another senseless killing. Always at the core of the tragedy is a lack of control. Perhaps in the old days, one would "get even" with a fist fight. Today, it is with a gun. I cringe when I think about how close I came to getting my gun and going back to shoot that security guard. As I ponder my jail time, perhaps that was the best thing that ever happened to me. It may have saved my life or someone else's life.

I never considered going to Europe to play basketball although that was certainly an option. I was married and had strong family roots in Detroit. I took on several jobs working with youth at places like the Don Bosco home and other government agencies. My marriage eventually dissolved, and I swore I would be a bachelor for the rest of my life. Hah!

Five years later, I renewed my relationship with Annette who had also been divorced. She was the love of my life and I of hers. She told me that she always knew that we would get back together. In junior high, I would ride my bike or walk the mile and a half to her house. On cold, snowy days, her mother would drive me back home. We went our separate ways in high school. I had other women as well as being addicted to my first love which was basketball.

Annette Marsh – what a woman! I can honestly say that she is my better half. Although just three of my children were by her, she has embraced all seven of them, not discriminating in any way, shape or form.

Not only is she my better half, but she is a prime example of opposites attract. Without writing about myself, I just want to tell about her. She is goal driven, optimistic, professional yet domesticated. She has a meal on the table Sunday through Thursday as well as working full time as an administrator at Detroit Receiving Hospital.

She is conscientious financially. She enjoys home decorating even being asked by other family members to help them in this regard. Even with my history, she is never jealous even having my ex-wife included at family gatherings. She is secure in herself.

Although she had never been interested in sports, after one of our sons played football, she became an avid NFL fan even putting on a Detroit Lions jersey or shirt on game days when the two of us are gathered on the couch to cheer on our team.

But most importantly, she was the prime motivator for me returning to get my college degree.

Thomas "Whitey" Daniels | white

I never had a thirty day jail sentence or dreams crushed while being on the verge of an NBA career. However, my career as a teacher was threatened by and eventually led to a five year sentence away from teaching. The culprit was the dreaded pink slip that indicated that several of our positions were not going to be renewed.

After eight years of teaching at Oakwood Junior High School in East Detroit, Michigan and having that threat at the end of three of the years, I was to be let go due to decreasing enrollment.

Just as a side note, East Detroit, which was a suburb just across Eight Mile Road, a road made famous or infamous by Eminem by the way, was later renamed Eastpointe to disassociate itself from the city of Detroit and its connotations.

What was I to do? I had four children. Up until this time, my life was well-scripted. I was a follower, mostly following in my brother's footsteps as far as education and career were concerned. Now, left to fend for myself, what was I to do?

Oakwood Junior High School was my home away from home. Great men like Al Bernardi, a gym teacher, football coach and mentor would be lost forever. George Smiley, one of my great friends, was also let go due to shrinking enrollment. He and I would tear it up at Oakwood, coaching football together and enjoying Happy Hour(or two or three) after school on Fridays. As the Temptations sang,

"Depressed and Down Hearted, I took to Cloud Nine." Now, I don't mean that I medicated myself with drugs and alcohol, although drinking was quite an option for me. I was in a fog; I was in a cloud. I was stressed and extremely worried.

Larry Seitz, my ex-brother-in-law was a successful business man who lived in all places, Rapid City, South Dakota. He offered me a position in manufactured homes sales that I could not refuse since I was in dire straights working for an insurance company in Southfield, Michigan.

I left my family to put down stakes in Rapid City. Eventually the family was reunited. Financially it worked out great. Larry was very generous and helped me a lot. Emotionally the move took its toll on all of us. After two years, we returned home, and I faced a broken marriage.

As Cookie related earlier, what doesn't kill you makes you stronger. I was devastated to the point of nearly being homeless with no real job and child support for four children. Except for the generosity of my good friends Dennis McMahon and George "Chick" Smiley who provided me a place to live, I could have been in an even tougher situation.

As a humorous interlude, George got his name from the smash series "Roots" in which a main character was named "Chicken George." Chick added to his nickname by one time bringing out a live chicken on a leash to one of our softball games. What was he supposed to bring, a turkey?

Anyway, through the grace of God, I survived two years of major difficulties and was rewarded by meeting my current wife, Joan, with whom I am celebrating our 33rd year of marriage and by being hired by Brother Rice High School in Bloomfield Hills, Michigan where I worked for thirty-two years. I was back on track, smarter and stronger and happier than ever.

Here I must relate the story of finding and courting Joan.

Sunday nights were difficult. Monday through Friday I worked selling industrial products over the phone for Mike McKeon, a good friend of mine. Friday nights were getting together with my friends for a beer or two or three or more. Saturdays and Sundays were devoted to my children trying to feed and entertain them on a pauper's budget. Sundays around 6:00 were when things got awkward and depressing. Then was when the reality of divorce would hit me.

As I have mentioned, I was never a confident man about town with women; my divorce did not change that. One Sunday after dropping off my children, I headed to a local bowling alley bar to meet up with Spider and Dan Rove to watch the football game. When I walked into the dark bar area, no one had arrived yet.

I did not notice the bar maid until I asked the question, "Where's the men's room?" The young woman looked up and pointed. I followed the directions, but the sight of her made that the fastest trip to a men's room in all documented history. She made an impression. Even at a distance, I could see those dark eyes, beautiful deep brown soulful eyes that a man could get lost in as I have over the years. She was tall but not taller than I. She had, and still has, a creamy complexion that never required much make up. And she had this just right nicely put together totally feminine form.

I did not talk to her much that first night. Instead, I watched. Still not very confident at this point in time, I did not ask her for her phone number.

I made it a habit to swing by the bowling alley bar almost every Sunday night. Suddenly, Sunday nights were not so lonely and depressing anymore. Spider, Dan, and the football game were not the attractions.

I found out that before her shift she would come to the snack bar and have a coffee. I made it a point to be there with coffee in hand, coffee with cream and sugar, just the way I liked it. Oops, she liked it black but kindly never complained.

Over the weeks I learned that she was not just a very pretty face. She was funny and smart. She was a hard worker, working six and seven days per week plus overtime any chance she could. She was divorced with two small boys and very fortunate to have her mother help watch them.

She was the kind of girl that scared me to death. Pretty, self-assured and not lacking in attention from the other men around the bar, but she did not have a boyfriend and was not trying to find one. Why I thought I had a shot with her is anyone's guess. I wasn't sure she would ever be interested in me, but I was absolutely smitten. That strong attraction was the catalyst that propelled me to ask her out that first time.

The event was a Detroit Lions game. Some of you may recall that a players' strike cancelled games that year causing the last game of the season to be postponed to January 2nd with the Green Bay Packers. (Lions squeaked out a 27 to 24 win to get into the playoffs.) George Smiley and a date along with another couple were attending that game as well. I asked her to go with me and to my utter amazement, she accepted. I was thinking that she must be a diehard Lions' fan but found out sometime later that she was a Washington Redskins' fan. Later in those playoffs the Skins beat the Lions. She was happy.

The divorce left me with very little, and since the family needed the van to transport my children, it stayed with the house. I had to find a car that I could afford. A good friend Gene Grewe told me that his recently deceased father-in-law had a car that they were trying to unload.

Taking out a loan from the East Detroit Employees Credit Union, I was styling in my $22 per month 1972 Plymouth Fury. I use the term styling sarcastically. The year was 1983. The Fury had no heat, but it did have a small rust hole on the floor of the passenger side. The Fury was serviceable for me to get back and forth from work. I did not think much more about it until I realized that I had a date with this beautiful woman. I panicked.

True, we had been getting to know each other over several weeks, but she did not know how hand to mouth my existence really was. I decided that she needed to understand that it would not be a 1983 Lincoln Continental pulling up to her door. If she backed out of the date, then she backed out.

This was stressful. Was I going to lose the woman that was becoming so important to me? I didn't know but needed to find out. I put it off as long as possible, but decided it's now or never. I went to the bowling alley when she got out of work to show her my car. I had a bit of liquid courage to fortify myself as a means of taking the chill off. It was a very cold night with no heat in the car, well you get the picture. I went into the bar to explain myself but couldn't make any sense. I decided that one picture would stand for the thousand words. I led her to the copper gold 1972 Plymouth Fury and opened the door to point out the hole and mentioned that the car had no functioning heater.

I held my breath trying to read her face. She looked up at me with eyebrows knitted together and asked, "Are you trying to sell me your car? Is this like a disclosure?"

I assured her that I only wanted her to understand that this would be the vehicle that I'd be driving for our date. She looked at me, took my hand and said, "I wanted to go out with you, not your car. Truly, I do not remember anything more about that night. I was dizzy. I was giddy. I was thrilled.

The night before our first date was New Years Day. Many friends and I were watching football all day long at Chicken George's house. It was a long night as well. The next day I was fuzzy and slow moving. I did everything that I could think of to get myself in shape for that day's long anticipated date. By 11:00 a.m., I was among the living once more. I decided that no date of mine was going to ride in a dirty car even if it had no heat. I went to the car wash on Gratiot and ended up in a long line. Shit, I was going to be late for my first date.

She wasn't happy and said that she was just about to call to see if she could work that evening since she was pretty sure that I had just stood her up. God, if she only knew. I am never, not ever, late. Fortunately, I got there before she made other plans, and she came along in the decade old, freezing cold, holey Fury. I wrapped her in a blanket, tucking my precious cargo in with all the care I could. Laughing at the time, she was grateful for the warmth by the time we got to the Silverdome.

The evening went great and solidified my opinion of her. She did two things that made me want her all the more. She waited for me while I used the men's room. Now that might seem like a very insignificant thing, but it was a consideration that I appreciated. The other thing was that after she won one of the bets we had going about the quarters' final scores, she was the first to buy the group a round of drinks. One of my buddies commented on how pretty she was but warned, "High maintenance, she looks like high maintenance." If I didn't know before that night, I now knew she wasn't.

After we married in September of 1983, I lamented that I wanted to take her out to concerts and theaters but could only afford a six pack of beer on a Saturday night. She kissed me and said that she needed to do laundry on Saturday nights. She would rather stay home and have a beer and match socks with me than be anywhere else. I thought she was nuts but grateful for her insanity.

Shortly after we were married, I got a job offer for another sales position. My work life for the past four years after leaving teaching was solely about earning money. She knew me better than I knew myself. "Is this the kind of work you want to do?" I told her it was sales, and I was becoming a pretty good salesman. She rephrased the question, "Is it the kind of work you like to do?" That was an easy question to answer. The kind of work that I loved to do was teaching. I wasn't just good at it, I was great at it, and I missed it every day. I explained that there were just no teaching jobs available. "Have you been applying for them?" Okay, she had me there.

That was in October, and by late December, 1983 I had a job offer from Brother Rice High School. Catholic school teachers are paid significantly less than public school teachers. I knew that taking this position would mean less income. My bride said, "You aren't in this alone. You've got me. Take the teaching job."

Those first few years of our marriage were tough. She went to work selling for New York Carpet World. That meant long hours away from home, but the money allowed us to purchase a home closer to where my children lived. It was still a struggle, but she never wavered in her loyalty and love for me. She tells me that it has been a two way street, and I have always been there for her.

All I know is Joan has been my biggest supporter, my lover, and friend for over thirty-three years. And I am still bringing her coffee but now black coffee that I serve to her at home. I am the happiest of men.

CHAPTER 6
Peculiar Relatives

Thomas "Cookie" Marsh | *black*

I have some peculiar relatives; who doesn't? It is just a matter of degrees. Probably the best story was of my great uncle when he was a young man. Seemed he liked the dice and got caught up in a losing streak one day. He offered up the family cow for collateral. Now, mind you, the cow was sacred, not like in India or something, but the cow was a source of great sustenance for the family. Great uncle lost the cow in the dice game which was not even his to lose. The winner of the cow eventually showed up at the house to take away the cow. He never did retrieve his winnings. Rumor has it that a stern voice and the barrel of a shotgun discouraged the taking of the cow. I do not think my great uncle gambled much after that, at least not ever with the cow!

Another relative was fighting a battle with substance abuse. He was having a hell of a time shaking the addiction even leading him to crack cocaine. Down in Mississippi, he put up his father's car for collateral for some crack. Since everyone knew everyone down there, the drug dealer did not keep the car and brought it back to its rightful owner.

When Tom Daniels and I were brainstorming about peculiar relatives, we were surprised but maybe not shocked to find out that each of our families had some weirdos including child molesters, drunks, and addicts. Race isn't selective.

Thomas "Whitey" Daniels | white

We all have them, black or white; they haunt all our families from being skeletons in the closet to just oddballs. These are the quirky aunts, uncles, cousins, etc. who end up being the talk at gatherings and then sources of gossip for hours. These are the people whom you can hardly live with but also couldn't live without. Family gatherings would be pretty quiet without these weird creatures.

Uncle Walter: An entire chapter could be written about this odd duck. God rest his soul. Uncle Walter was a minister in some German church. Sad to say but we suspected him a Nazi though this was never substantiated nor was there ever any real indication that he was except that he was German. As kids, we had unfounded ideas. As a minister, he was true to his form giving the blessing before the meal. These were doozies to say the least. Again, our irreverent immaturity showed as his daughter, sons, nephews, and nieces could hardly restrain our silly laughter as he droned on with scriptural contemplations while the delicious food that he was praying over got cold.

At a gathering whether it be a joyous occasion or a solemn one, Uncle Walter remained constant. The fear was always: who would be "Uncle Waltered"? Each of us would occasionally take one for the team and spend an interminable thirty minutes being shown pictures of who knows whom. I surely didn't, nor did I care. If you looked up the definition of boring in the dictionary, you would surely see Uncle Walter there with a handful of nondescript photos with his victim glassy eyed and drooling trying to stay awake.

Please don't get me wrong. I loved Uncle Walter for the opportunities he afforded my parents to travel and get about. Believe it or not, my parents never drove a car. Uncle Walter, of course, did.

"Stiff Dick Walter" – when I heard my ex-brother-in-law place this nickname on Uncle Walter, I just about spit out the Boneyard Ribs that I was enjoying with my sister and my wife. Somehow, Uncle Walter got the reputation as quite the cock hound when it came to his wife Aunt Margaret. Just the visual of this skinny, old man chasing his plus sized wife into submission was enough to make us all lose it. Well, good for him. I am certain he did not need Viagra!

Speaking of Viagra and losing it, Cookie, Derek, Guy Edwards and I were going to a Detroit Tigers baseball game thanks to the generosity of Guy who was also driving the car. Somehow the conversation turned to Viagra. Without skipping a beat, Cookie exclaimed, "Viagra? Shit! Just give me some gin." We lost it right then and there.

CHAPTER 8

Careers

Thomas "Cookie" Marsh | black

As mentioned before, my career path took me into social work. You can imagine some of the strange and tragic stories that I could relate about these poor, afflicted souls. At one time, I was working at a mental hospital. This certain woman patient, let's call her Miss Smith, was always plotting how to escape. One evening she concocted a plan that was incredible.

There was a pay phone in the lobby, and I noticed that she was making a call. Now, mind you, we were basically on a first name basis with the owners of the funeral home around the block due to a variety of deaths such as drug overdoses, suicides, and just plain bad health. Well, the entryway doorbell rang that evening, and the usual men from the funeral home, equipped with a body bag and a stretcher, were at the door asking to remove the dead body of a Miss Smith.

You got it. The woman thought she could escape the institution by having the funeral parlor carry her out of there. Bad plan because as soon as they mentioned her name, I said that they must be mistaken because Miss Smith was standing right over there by the television set.

Tom Daniels and I have had great careers helping others which was a tremendously rewarding experience for both of us. But, as I mentioned before, my passion was for basketball, so it was only natural that I would end up coaching the sport. As Tom says, coaching is not about the wins and losses. Years later, who really cares? What matters are the memories. What matters are the joys and disappointments that shape lives.

After my freshman year at the University of Detroit, Dave Bing invited me to be a camp counselor at his basketball clinic in the Poconos in Pennsylvania. Dave, a Detroit Piston all-star who played with Bob Lanier for many years, was big in Pennsylvania having been an All-American at Syracuse University.

Just as a side note, Cazzie Russell was the star University of Michigan player who entered the NBA draft the same year as Dave Bing. Everyone in Michigan was hoping that Cazzie would join the Pistons. Because the Pistons and the New York Knicks had the same terrible record the year before, they were involved in a coin flip to determine who got the first pick. The Knicks won the flip and selected Cazzie Russell much to the huge disappointment of all Pistons fans. Not so fast! Cazzie Russell became an average NBA player, and Dave Bing became a perennial All-Star leading the Pistons out of the basement of the NBA to the penthouse.

Down the street from me lived a little guy by the name of Benny White. He was about thirteen years old and was pretty small for his age but a terrific basketball player. Benny somehow heard that I was going to Pennsylvania to work this basketball camp and relentlessly asked if he could go with me. Every day for a week, he would stand on my porch in the morning with his little suitcase to make sure that I would not leave without him.

The day of departure arrived. I went to his house to speak to his mother. She said it was all right and that she trusted me to take good care of her son. We were on our way for the 500 mile trek to the Poconos.

When we pulled into the facility, Dave Bing greeted me asking who was that kid with me. Now the cost of the camp for the week was $150. Dave asked me where is this kid going to stay and what is he going to eat knowing full well that Benny was not going to be a paid camper. I told him that Benny was going to stay in my room and that I would give him half of my food at every meal. Bing walked away saying okay.

For the first two days, Benny slept at the end of my bed and ate half of my meals. On the third day after what I believe were testing days by Bing to see if I would follow through on my promise, Dave Bing took notice of Benny White.

Benny excelled at the camp, and Dave Bing gave him his own room and his own food card. To this day nearly fifty years later, Dave Bing and Benny White are extremely close as Bing became like a second father to Benny. By the way, Benny went on to star at Michigan State University and has given back to the sport as the former coach of Martin Luther King High School in Detroit and now as an assistant coach at Eastern Michigan University.

Robert Taylor, my high school coach at Detroit Northern, became a second father to me. I was teased throughout high school by others probably jealous that Coach Taylor and I had such a strong bond. Thankfully that bond continued as I assisted him while he coached at Martin Luther King High School many years later.

I learned a lot from him and how to win games. He always said, "Get the ball to the shooter!" One time a boy who was not a good shooter challenged Coach Taylor stating after taking a missed shot, "But Coach, I was wide open." Coach responded quickly, calmly, and sternly, "Son, there is a reason why you were wide open; you are a poor shooter, and the defense wanted you to shoot." To this day, I make it a point to visit Coach regularly.

I coached girls but only for a year at St. Bridget Catholic Elementary School. What a trip as they say! I was eager to help because one of my cousin's daughters was on the team. On the very first day, I had to break up a fight because the defense, doing just what I asked them to do, were closely guarding the offensive players. All I heard was, "She's too close; she needs to back off." Then all hell broke loose. I actually coached girls twice: my first and last time!

Although coaching was great for the most part, unfortunately the specter of racism and discrimination reared its ugly head.

Harold Lowe and I were assisting Jerry Guinane at a suburban Catholic high school. Jerry was and still is a terrific instructor who can train all levels making anyone a better athlete and basketball player. We had a good team that was getting better until some parents intervened causing the administration to relieve us of our coaching duties. The official reason was that we were not supervising the locker room area. We knew, however, that the true reason was that we were playing a couple of black kids over some white kids.

Now mind you that Jerry is white and Harold and I are black. We stated in the book earlier that it didn't matter if you were black or white, as long as you could play the game and had a good attitude you were welcome.

The fact of the matter here was that the two black players at this predominantly white school on this predominantly white team were better than most of the white players. Some white parents could not accept that their sons were just not good enough and pulled out the race card pressuring the administration to fire us.

Another difficult situation reared itself when I was coaching with Benny White at Martin Luther King in the late 1990s. We had a strength and conditioning coach by the name of "Sarge" because he was a retired military man. Sarge would often show up to practice with scratches on his face and arms. One day we had to actually postpone practice because Coach White was trapped in his office becoming a marriage counselor to Sarge and his wife.

At the end of the season, we were down at Cobo Arena getting ready for the Public School League championship game. Sarge was supposed to bring the uniforms. We waited and waited getting more nervous by the minute. Now remember, this was a time way before cell phones, so communication was difficult. We got hold of someone at the school, and a janitor brought us the uniforms just in the nick of time. You guessed it; Sarge had gotten into a fight with his wife and lost track of all time. So much for Coach White's counseling abilities.

But for the most part, coaching was about relationships and watching the players develop into good adults. James Theus, who was runner-up to Marcus Taylor out of Lansing Waverly for Mr. Basketball, became a celebrated DJ in the Atlanta, Georgia area. He was a quiet, reserved young man, but away from the court he had a different passion. He developed his DJ skills at school dances and local clubs. We learn that very few of these players go on to careers as NBA players. As they say in that wonderful commercial sponsored by the NCAA, "We go pro in a lot of areas besides sports."

Thomas "Whitey" Daniels | white

I also mentioned earlier that I was in education for nearly forty years. And again, parallel lines crossed with Cookie as both of us ended up coaching basketball. I coached over a period of 25 years or more ranging from 8th and 9th grade boys to JV boys to Varsity boys to Varsity girls. What a trip! To say that winning championships would be the highlight of my career would be a lie.

We enjoyed two JV league championships at U of D High thanks to great players like Tim Anderson, Don Fucinari, Ron Robinson, Ron Budd, Ed Moultrie, Derrick Mayes, and Kyle King just to name a few, and two league championships coaching the Girls Varsity at Rochester Adams thanks again to great players like the Newsom twins Lexy and Whitney, Amber Jamison, Lauren Boyle, Jenny Rosanke, Ravin Owusu, Taylor Houghtlin, and the Finklestine sisters Nicki and Lauren.

As with Cookie and the mental health stories and my working with teenage boys for so long, there are certainly hundreds of interesting if not crazy stories to relate. Those, however, will have to wait for a future book. For now I would like to stick with basketball related stories.

Here we go:

If I had the stereotype that all blacks can play basketball, early in my coaching career this myth was destroyed. A sophomore, let's call him Eric, was a big, strong, athletic looking young man. In tryouts, I said to myself that we really have a chance with Eric on the inside for us. We had very few practices before our first game. And hope sprang eternal even though Eric caught the basketball with his face more often than with his hands. I kept saying that as long as he could rebound and defend the low post, we would be all right.

In the pre-season tournament game held over at Dondero High School, all hope for Eric was lost. He was running the floor on a fast break; the ball was passed to him; of course he dropped it before he could make an easy layup, but then the worst happened. We went back on defense with four players. Where was Eric? There were exit doors at the end of the gym. He could not put on the brakes after that mishandled fast break and ended up going through the doors that locked behind him. My dilemma was to let him back in or just let him keep on going.

Often, the laugh is on the coach. If you do not have a sense of humor about yourself as a teacher, social worker, or a coach, you are sure to be a miserable person. It is a good thing that I did in the following situation.

At Brother Rice coaching the JV team, we were in a losing streak which was something we were not accustomed to considering we had the likes of Mike Radlick, Mike Cappetto (Duke football QB), and Charlie Gant (MSU tight end). I was in a fiery mood along with my son Josh who was my assistant coach. We had just dropped our third game in a row – totally unacceptable.

Well, I went up to the white board in the locker room and in no uncertain terms wrote out all the glaring errors that we were making, calling out the culprits as I raged on. No one escaped this rampage. Trying to end this ten minute tirade on a positive note, my plan was to erase all the transgressions that filled the board to illustrate the point that those games were in the past. We will start anew. We will not play like that anymore.

Not so fast, coach! What I did not realize was that I had written with permanent markers and not dry erase markers. One swipe of the board and I knew I was doomed. Not so fast! Hearing the players begin to snicker, I quickly regained my composure and roared, "Obviously, these mistakes that you have been making are not that easy to get rid of. See you at practice tomorrow and be ready to run."

With that, Josh and I went out the back door that led to the parking lot and laughed until we cried.

Another "laugh is on the coach" story involved a commercial being shot to promote the Volkswagen Vanagon. Somehow, probably because our Brother Rice basketball team was taller than the Detroit Pistons that year with twin seven footers and others above 6'5", Volkswagen wanted to show how great its van was being able to accommodate a lot of large people.

We assembled at Manresa Retreat House at Quarton and Woodward in Bloomfield Hills for the shoot. Somehow I was elected to park the car in a narrow space between two parked cars. After about five takes and a few scratched and dented bumpers, I was relieved of my driving duties. I can still hear Dan Ervin, one of our taller players snickering as I attempted this impossible feat. By the way, after another driver took over for me, they widened the parking space.

Coaching girls, let's just say, is a different experience. I loved every minute of it, but it was a complete culture shock from coaching the boys.

For example, on my first day of practice we were going over offense when Lauren Zielinski, our point guard and captain of the team, stopped, put the ball on the floor between her feet and started scratching her legs. I asked her what she was doing. She calmly stated that she had a lot of mosquito bites and had to scratch them.

Now let me tell you, if this had happened at a boys varsity practice, that player would have been taken out of the practice, sent home or would run until he learned his lesson to not interrupt the flow of practice.

Another quirk, shall we say, was uncovered at the end of the season at our banquet. Apparently, during games or at practices when a girl would make a mistake and was obviously feeling bad about it, the reaction from one or another player would be, "That's okay, at least you're pretty!"

I really learned a lesson from the absolute worst team that I ever coached. I took on the 8th grade boys' team at Kelly Junior High in East Detroit. After coaching at U of D High and being relatively successful there, I was eager and even cocky thinking that I could develop a good team at Kelly. After the first practice, I was concerned when one of the players crashed into the drinking fountain some distance away from the court splitting his head open and having to go off for stitches. By the way, this was my best player. Patiently, I endured the season and almost beat the team from Mt.Clemens that hadn't lost a game in years. We finished the season winning zero games and losing ten. At a small banquet at the end of the year, I received a trophy that I still cherish to this day. The inscription read, "Thanks, Coach Daniels for a Great Season" and then down below it read, "10 and 0: who said that the wins have to come first!"

Cookie mentioned some racial issues that he had with coaching. I guess it goes along with the territory; however, I got it from both directions white and black.

Kevin Wickliffe, may God rest his soul, eventually became like an adopted son to me. I will never forget the day he entered the Kimball High School gym during pre-season conditioning sometime in October around 1990. He quickly showed that he had the potential to be the best player in our entire program. I promoted him from the JV to the Varsity early in the season much to the chagrin of Coach Gordie Lindsay who saw his team crash and burn after losing Kevin. Kevin was one of a handful of black players in the entire basketball program. Needless to say, many of the white parents whose sons were losing playing time were none to happy with Coach Daniels.

A crazy story happened concerning Kevin early in his senior season. We had a decent team, and we were definitely hoping for a .500 season. Therefore, every victory was huge for us. We were playing at Hazel Park that Friday, and even though they had a terrific player in Irwin Marchand who eventually played at Wayne State University, I thought we could win. I pumped up Wickliffe all week urging him to accept the challenge between him and Marchand. We were ready; I was pumped up.

Not so fast, Coach D. Kevin absolutely stunk up the gym, and we lost by twenty. When we got back to the school, I was livid and blasted Wickliffe to no end even telling him not to return to practice. Now remember, this was the same kid that I drove home every day after practice and whom I counseled regularly as he did not have a father and his mother had issues.

A day or two passed, and Kevin came in to see me very apologetically. I was not prepared for what he had to say. After school before that game, Kevin had his first sexual experience. He told me that he could not focus being so filled with so many emotions. I was speechless and hugged him. No coaching clinic, seminar or book had ever touched on a situation like that.

Another racial issue occurred when a black mother unloaded on me because she knew that the only reason her son was not getting playing time was because I was a racist. While she was condemning me, little did she know that I had a black ex-player living in my home in Warren, Michigan while he was going through some difficult times. It is too bad when people pull the race card when they are disappointed and can not accept the truth. Her son was just not good enough to play.

In conclusion, as Cookie mentioned, coaching is about developing relationships and watching our players turn into productive members of society.

Only a few such as BJ Armstrong who starred at Brother Rice, the University of Iowa, and the Chicago Bulls fulfill that dream of an NBA career. It wasn't a surprise that BJ ascended to the NBA with a great work ethic being never late to school and always the first to practice and the last to leave. This work ethic eventually got him drafted by the Chicago Bulls playing alongside Michael Jordan. He developed into a great three point shooter because as Jordan and Scottie Pippen penetrated, BJ set up for the three pointer carrying him to the NBA All-Star game one year.

Although I never directly coached BJ, I was on the coaching staff when he played, graduating in 1985. Nick Conti, Frank Carrico and I traveled to the University of Iowa to visit with BJ and to learn from his coach George Raveling and later Dr. Tom Davis. What a thrill it was to be warmly welcomed there.

Other relationships included Pete Mitchell from Brother Rice, Boston College, and the Jacksonville Jaguars. I taught Pete junior English and still remember the poster he made about "What Everyone Should Know about British Literature." Pete gathered up a few of his muscular teammates his senior year in high school and actually helped my family move to a different home.

Another lifelong relationship is with Scott Newman whom I coached at Brother Rice and continue to see and support as he pursues his dream of being a high school coach himself.

The story of coaching basketball would not be complete without mentioning the colorful, dedicated, and talented men that I learned from and admired: Dan Hafner, Uof D High; Nick Conti, Brother Rice,; Frank Carrico, Brother Rice; Bill Norton, Brother Rice; Jimmy Carron, Kimball High; Chuck Jones, Kimball High; Gordie Lindsay, Kimball High; Mike Lewis, Kimball High; Josh Daniels, Brother Rice; Fran Scislowicz, Rochester Adams High.

All of these men had unique skills in teaching the game of basketball. They shared, however, the common ingredient: passion. This passion was not only for their sport but also for their players.

Coaching should be pure and color blind. If you are better than the others, if you are not a whiner, if you do not have too large of an ego, you will play. Someone asked me one time, "How many black players do you have on your team?" I looked at him with disbelief. I responded, "Who knows and who cares." If only that were true in society as a whole.

CHAPTER 9
Conclusion

While Tom Daniels and I were in Mississippi one early morning sharing the same hotel room at the beautiful Beau Rivage Casino and Resort, we began to freely talk about a number of sensitive issues. This was a clearing of the air, so to speak. We found out immediately that this open conversation is just what is needed to understand each other's viewpoint not just for us, but also for everyone. The following are some of the topics we discussed:

COOKIE & WHITEY

MEDIA

Every morning and, for that matter, every evening the lead story on the local news is the murder, fire (arson), carjacking, rape, abduction, or any other heinous act perpetrated in Detroit.

I asked Cookie what he thought a white person's perspective would be on hearing and seeing these reports. I told him that all these stories did were to perpetuate the fear and disgust for and ignorance of African-Americans with such comments as "What kind of animals live in that city?" Why do the media continue to cover these events? Cookie said it best, "Ratings. They are either clueless or are intentionally trying to divide the races."

Consider the report from Charleston, South Carolina that showed the white and black communities coming together after the senseless shootings in a black church by a deranged, ignorant white man. The original story of violence was covered in depth over a period of days. The story of healing and togetherness was a blip on the screen. Why? Ratings!

Think about the rioting in Ferguson, Missouri and Baltimore, Maryland, headlines for weeks if not months. Again, what do you think a white person's perspective on these riots was? I will tell you bluntly: absolute disgust and anger for the police involved in the unfair treatment of the black citizens; absolute disgust and anger for the looting and destruction of property and the damaging of the city.

How can blacks and whites learn to trust each other when these reports are in our faces every day? You are what you eat, and if this is what you consume on a daily basis, your soul is going to suffer from malnutrition.

It has been interesting to me about how many things I assumed were fact but weren't, and how many things I thought I knew that

I didn't really know. I suspect this is true of all of us because of religious, cultural and racial differences. However, sometimes, maybe even most times, it is divisive, and the worst part is that it usually sounds so innocent. Take a close look at the following stereotypes. By communicating and interacting with the other race, these walls may be broken down.

CP TIME

In another world a million miles away, the term "colored person" was a step up from other much less savory names. I don't know where it falls today. I suspect that it is probably just an old-fashioned colloquialism. The way I heard it most was in connection with CP time or colored person time. For those persons who were late, the label CP was securely affixed. Did it make anyone more likely to be early? Nope. It just annoyed them. Yeah, not too productive.

A Geezerball player named George was the poster child for CP Time. If basketball started at 1:00 as it often did on Saturday afternoons at Brother Rice High School, George would show up at 2:00 regularly. You could almost set your watch to it. Usually by 3:00 the rest of us geezers had enough of basketball and were ready to quit, tired and out of energy. Inevitably, George would be upset wondering why we were stopping so early. Geez!

On the other hand, another geezer Gene Seaborn was always early. I one time drew his attention to the difference between him and George. Gene said, "I am aware of the stigma of CP Time. I do not want anyone to think less of me and my son Chad by continuing that characterization of black people."

By the way, Derek Palm who has helped with the writing of this book and who has provided the Afterword, is always on time as well. Now Cookie Marsh? Let's just say his timeliness fluctuates. Cookie's deceased father would inform the family that they were leaving for Mississippi at 7:00 a.m. Cookie's mother would have everything packed and the food cooked and ready to go by 6:30 a.m. The car rolled out of the driveway at 3:00 p.m.

As for me? I am always early. My deceased mother was the type of person who would be all dressed and sitting on the front porch thirty minutes before she was to be picked up. As I mentioned earlier, my father would be just in the nick of time everyday for work.

Now, keep in mind that CP Time also applies to white people. Did you know that? We all have in our white families some people who are chronically late. Tell them 2:00 for dinner; see them at 3:30. Ask them what would be a comfortable time to come over for the barbecue, and they would request for instance 4:00. We all knew better not to start the ribs on the grill until 5:00.

CP Time is not a black thing. It is a people thing. Some people are early; some are in-time, and some are late.

BLACK PEOPLE FOOD

Watermelon and ribs. I have heard too many times that black people like watermelon and ribs as if this was some sort of a put down. I don't get it. Who doesn't like watermelon and especially ribs? Heck, I even know an older Jewish woman who told me she was risking going to hell because she likes ribs so much. My son-in-law Jimmy who is married to my daughter Jessy in North Carolina makes the most mouthwatering ribs to die for. Now Jimmy is a southern man who grew up during the times of great racial discrimination in the South. He loves and makes ribs. Sorry there, African-Americans, we whiteys love ribs as well. Can someone pass the watermelon, fried chicken, and grits?

WHITE MEN CAN'T JUMP

Apparently no one ever told Larry Birkett this. Larry is white, went to St. Gregory's along with my good friend and fellow geezer Jimmy Carron. Larry could glide through the air with the best of them as he made his mark on men's leagues throughout metropolitan Detroit.

In our coaching careers, we have seen many blacks who could neither jump nor play basketball very well. Just as we have seen whites who were good and bad. For certain, the sport of basketball is now dominated by blacks, and we all appreciate their amazing skills. But to say because you are black, you are a better basketball player than a white is ridiculous.

However, many people, black and white, would ignorantly profess this. Come out to Geezerball sometime. There are very good black players and very good white players. We believe that Geezerball is a microcosm of the real world. Cookie related his encounters with very good white players through Boys Club tournaments, summer leagues, and college.

PENISES & SHRINKAGE

Who can forget the Seinfeld episode when George literally got caught with his pants down by a woman who barged into the room where he was changing? According to George, he had shrinkage due to the cold water of the ocean that he had been swimming in.

Do black men have bigger penises than white men? Well that is another stereotype that we white men have suffered with forever. Although my sample size of black penises is far less than that of white penises, I can say that the largest penises I saw were those of white men. However, after learning from Cookie about a basketball team mate of his who had the nickname "Moby Dick", I am not so sure.

I do know that I had a George Costanza like experience not too long ago after playing tennis. I usually wear compression shorts when participating in physical activity. Well, you guessed it, much more got compressed than my hamstrings and quads. I did not realize how compressed until I got in the shower and had to forcibly dig that ole boy out. Walking through the locker room on my way to the shower probably made that stereotype real and men in there happy they were not me. Shit!

ASHY

I couldn't help but laugh out loud when I first heard one of the black players who I coached on the JV basketball team at U of D High School in the 1970s say he was all ashy asking if anyone had some skin lotion. What a perfect description for that flaky, dry skin that covers dark colored socks making it look like you just walked through a snow bank.

Got news for you African-Americans, whites have that affliction as well. This is probably not a black or white thing but a cold weather thing. Living in Michigan with the furnace's dry heat wreaks havoc on all humans' skin. Dry skin even occurs in the summer time especially in low humidity climates. Heck, I even have to add olive oil to the dogs' food in the winter time to stop their itching and flaking.

BROTHERHOOD

Cookie and I forged a togetherness beginning as almost total strangers to now being called "brothers from other mothers." In this day and age of superficiality (can anyone say, "Facebook Friends"), does anyone really get to know another person let alone a person from another race, ethnic group, or religion?

We have a black President in the United States of America. Did anyone ever believe that this would be possible not for just one term but now two? We have a white Mayor in the city of Detroit which is 90% black. Yet, why is there so much racial unrest and distrust? Obviously, neither President Obama nor Mayor Dugan could have been elected with straight black or white votes.

An iceberg is only about twenty percent above water. Very little of its enormity can be seen from above. (Ask the Titanic if you do not believe me.) While Cookie and I contemplated this fact, we could not help comparing icebergs to people. Yet, we constantly judge people only by what they look like.

I must admit that men as a group are quite shallow this way. We are constantly judging women by how they look. I am not sure how much of this women do, but from my viewpoint of women, I believe they do less of it. Thank God, or we would never have had a date or even gotten married!

On July 2, 2015, Cookie and Tom took a trip to Laurel, Mississippi by way of a gambling junket to the Beau Rivage Casino and Resort in Biloxi. From the long abandoned diner that would not serve "niggers" to the Friendship Road to the segregated swimming pool, we forged a closer bond.

Cookie let me see under his water, so to speak, to uncover the rest of his iceberg. We visited with several family members and saw where he played as a kid taking many pictures. Sharing this trip reinforced that we were really no different. We both had relatives who loved us no matter the distance or time away who remain the fiber of our lives.

Certainly Cookie and I disagree on a variety of topics: he votes straight Democrat and I lean toward Republican; he respected Muhammad Ali's conscientious objection, and I questioned it. So what? We both respect each other's viewpoints and are able to openly discuss them.

There was an old song by the Dramatics called "Whatcha You See is Whatcha You Get." The Dramatics was a Detroit group, and the lead singer Ron Banks (RIP) was an acquaintance of Cookie's. Now, this title may be true only if you see part of the iceberg. How many people really take the time to learn all about a person? It is very easy to say, "Do something," but without showing or explaining how to do something, those words are really quite useless.

How can people see the eighty percent of each other that is not on the surface?

There was a great Broadway musical and subsequent movie called *The King and I* starring Yul Bryner and Julie Andrews. One of the featured tunes was "Getting to Know You":

> Getting to know you, getting to know all about you
> Getting to like you, getting to hope you like me.

Here are a few suggestions as to how to begin to do this:

TRAVELING

Just recently on a cruise ship to Bermuda, my wife and I had the good fortune to be seated at dinner across from a black lady from Philadelphia who, we learned, was a retired school principal. I enjoyed the conversation learning we had a lot in common as I too was a school administrator.

But the most important and odd thing about the conversation was when she told us of her trip to Russia. Our generation grew up distrusting or even hating the Russians. The Cold War was part of our existence, and the Cuban Missile Crisis was traumatic.

Continuing the meeting with this fine lady, she indicated with great surprise how kind and helpful the Russian people that she had encountered were. I could not help thinking that while she was talking about the Russians, I, as a white man, was thinking about similar encounters that I have had with blacks who were equally pleasant.

Ignorance causes prejudice; it is as simple as that. As Atticus said in To Kill a Mockingbird, "Until you climb into another's shoes and walk around in them, you will never know what he or she is like."

I never tried on Cookie's shoes (they would be too big for me literally and figuratively), but in getting to know this man, I certainly understand him and call him my friend!

READING

The very fact that you are reading our book is helping you to see things about blacks and whites that you may never have realized. Many other books would be beneficial as well, such as To Kill a Mockingbird and Black Like Me. I can never forget that ironic scene in TKaM when the Ladies Auxiliary was sewing clothing to be sent to Africa for the destitute there when blacks in their own home of Maycomb, Alabama were being discriminated against and falsely accused of crimes they did not commit.

CONVERSING

In the introduction, we wrote about Sundays/Saturdays being the most segregated days of the week: the Sabbath, the Lord's Day. When is the last time you actually had a conversation with a member of a different race or ethnic background? The main purpose of our book is to begin a movement that starts with open conversations with the other race. Fear and ignorance are crippling and lead to close-mindedness and stereotypical opinion.

This movement begins with embracing opportunities to get to know all about others.

EPILOGUE
Derek Palm

After reading *Black and White Like You and Me* the story of two young boys one black and one white growing up in the city of Detroit in the 1950s and 1960s, I could not help but review my own childhood and life.

The story shows how "Parallel Lines Sometimes Intersect." Tom (Cookie) Marsh and Tom (Whitey) Daniels, because they grew up in different parts of Detroit, you might think that their lives would never intertwine. Their childhood experiences would seem to be entirely different. But were they really that unalike?

As they grew into their teens and adulthood, a common interest had taken form in both of their lives. That interest was athletics. Cookie was becoming a star basketball player in high school and the University of Detroit while Tom was a good baseball player at the University of Detroit with a developing love for basketball.

Ahhh! Here it is that intersecting common interest – athletics and basketball – that brings these two Detroits together. As mentioned early in the book, the two now older men began playing basketball together. As they began to develop a friendship on and off the court, conversations eventually led to the writing of this book. A major development was the racial discussion that brought the two even closer together. In the racially and politically charged environment that we find ourselves in today, more of these open discussions are necessary.

In case you are wondering who I am, I am an African-American who grew up in Detroit during the same time period as Cookie and Tom. My "parallel lines" intersected with them later in life as well in 2008. It was also basketball that brought us together. Although I have gotten to know both through playing together, they have become good friends off the court. We continue to have great discussions regarding family, life, politics, racial issues, etc. Quite frankly, I wish this type of forum could be done on a larger, even national scale. Many times, simple questions and verbalizing concerns can clear up stereotypes and misconceptions.

Therefore, what do we learn from *Black and White Like You and Me*? We are all different and unique, but we are all still the same. As the Temptations sang in the 1970s, "Look in the mirror, what do you see? Two eyes, a nose, and a mouth just like me." If you look at the world of athletics and music, people do not care about race, sex, or ethnic background. All that matters is can you play the game or do you have musical ability.

In conclusion, some say that your life flashes before your eyes just before you die if only for a few seconds. After my reading of *Black and White Like You and Me*, I have had continuous flashbacks of my life with very fond memories that have provided me with continuous smiles. They say that a good book, song, or movie is one that makes you think and feel long after the actual experience of the reading, hearing, or viewing. I know that this book has had the same effect on all of us.

DEREK PALM

AUTHORS' NOTE

We asked Derek and Spider to be our consultants during our writing journey. We thought it only appropriate that our readers get to know these two men. We know that the addition of their short biographies, although each of them were on such a roll it was hard for them to make them short, will further illustrate the common bonds that we all have.

This triggering of memories which call to mind so many anecdotes both happy and sad is the very same reaction we hope you will have after reading our book.

BIOGRAPHY | DEREK PALM

I was born in Detroit, but my earliest childhood memories begin in the early 1950s in Highland Park, Michigan, a small city completely surrounded by the city of Detroit. The neighborhood I grew up in was nice, mostly four family flats with lots of kids and everyone knew each other.

My favorite memory was when I asked for a horseshoe set after getting straight A's on my report card. I became the horseshoe king of the block. We spent hours during summer days playing horseshoes on the side of the apartment building. I would always have pocket change due to those foolish enough to challenge me, even the fathers!

After fifth grade we moved to northwest Detroit in the Wyoming and McNichols(6 Mile) area. I will never forget my first day at my new school, Schultz Elementary. Being a new student, I was in class early (no CP Time for me) to meet my new homeroom teacher. When the students entered the classroom, white and mostly Jewish, they surrounded my desk showing great excitement and curiosity to see me. As I look back, it must have seemed to them like bringing home a new puppy to a house full of children. My new classmates were very accepting of me: wanting to be friends, wanting to eat lunch with me, playing baseball and basketball after school. I was often invited to their homes after school for study and play. I later came to find out that I was just the third black in the entire school.

I have been teased that my family was the black version of *Leave It to Beaver*. As for my family, I lived with my mother, father and a younger brother. My father became the top Buick salesman in the Metro Detroit area. He was the first black salesman for that company as well. My mother was a top fashion designer and model who made clothing for some of the local recording artists including Motown greats like Gladys Knight, Martha Reeves, Aretha Franklin, and the Temptations to name a few. My parents were doing quite well financially as they moved to Southfield just after I graduated from Mumford in 1970.

It was during the 70s that I began to show my basketball prowess. I had a basketball scholarship to Mercy College in Detroit that later became partnered with the University of Detroit. As I improved my skills, in the summer we would travel the city in order to play against the best competition. St. Cecilia, Brewster Projects, outside courts at U of D, and Peterson Park attracted top players from all over the city. It was during these games that you could run into Cookie Marsh, a star player at Northern High and later at the University of Detroit.

As you can see, my parallel line probably runs right in the middle of Tom's and Cookie's. Here is where they intersect due to sports especially basketball. Even today at our age, our love for the game keeps us playing as much as possible. We have all learned from the game, and it has helped us with the game of life. We have met through basketball, but have become friends outside of basketball. I am sure we all would agree that it has helped us with our jobs, as husbands, fathers and so on. I am thankful to have intersected with Cookie and Tom. I am delighted to have become part of this important project.

BIOGRAPHY | BOB "SPIDER" DANIELS

Much of what my early years were like was consistent to my brother's with the exception that I am a little over a year older than Tom. Even though, just like Derek, I could go on forever conjuring up the memories of my childhood, I am going to limit myself to what I call part three of my life, my teaching career.

On the 3rd of September, a day I will always remember (sound familiar to the Temptations' "Poppa Was a Rollin' Stone"?) , the phone rang on our black rotary phone. A man on the other end of the line wanted to know if Robert Daniels was there. He asked me if I wanted to teach in Detroit at Sherrard Junior High. I would be an English teacher taking the place of a Dr. Rheaume. Without hesitation, I answered, "Yes." With a big sigh of relief, he said, "Thank you" and hung up. All I knew was that the school was located at 8300 Cameron. I was so excited that I didn't even ask what the grade levels were or what time school started. Grabbing the trusty DSR Bus Route Book, I mapped out my way to 8300 Cameron, no GPS back then. I would take Gratiot down to Harper, turn right past East Town Theater to East Grand Boulevard then right past St. Joseph Hospital to the I-75 service drive and then left onto Clay Avenue and right on to Cameron Street.

Little did I know what I was getting into. Bright eyed and bushy tailed at the ripe old age of twenty-two, I walked into the school. The first person that I met was the janitor. "Who are you?" he barked. "I am the new English teacher," I responded. His reply was short and to the point, "We don't need none." Well, that's how the first day of thirty-three years began. The previous deep sigh of the personnel director and the surprising words of the janitor were just some clues of what lay ahead for me.

It took years to convince the Sherrard community that I really belonged there. Suspicious, stereotypes, distrust, and hatred grow deep especially shortly after the Civil Disturbance of 1967 (the Riots). Sherrard was an all-black school in an all-black neighborhood on the north end of the Black Bottom. The scars of segregation, poverty, and despair permeated everything. The last thing this Region One Area D wanted was another white face to teach their black children. I was the last of those white faces hired as the sixties ended, and the seventies began.

Cookie could tell you from a student's point of view how an inner city junior high operated. I can give you my perspective from a teacher's point of view. It isn't pretty.

I know that I learned plenty from my 33 years at Sherrard. I only hope that my students learned half as much as I did. I always tried to do more than teach. I ran an after school recreation program from day one. Coaching the 7th and 8th grade basketball team as the kids say "was a trip." I worked in the junior high lunchroom for twenty-five years. Again, ask Cookie what that must have been like. I read off more words than I can recount working with the Spelling Bee for 32 years.

I have to pause here to tell of the time when one of my best spellers ever attended the area-wide Spelling Bee. We were all excited; her parents, grandparents, and other family members were in attendance. Tension ran high as we were expecting victory. The young lady was that good. In order to relax the contestants and make sure the speaker system and judges were in order, each contestant was given an easy warm up word to make sure of procedures. Well, her warm up word was "chicken." In a quivering voice that resonated through the auditorium, she began, "Chicken, c-h-i-k-a-n." Her supporters including me fell back into our seats and closed our eyes. Needless to say, she did not get past the first round. The poor girl was devastated; nerves had gotten the best of her.

I was also in charge of graduation for most of my years there. Other jobs included acting counselor, assistant principal, and black history coordinator. In my last ten years, I was in charge of the school improvement plan. Don't hold that against me. It seemed like I was on every committee, went to every seminar, field trip, as well as giving seminars of my own to the staff. The black counselor referred to me as "HNIC" Head Negro in Charge! (Remember, I'm a white guy.)

In 1974, Zodie Johnson was sent by the Board of Education to straighten up Sherrard. At her former school Marxhausen, she had raised reading levels from second grade to high school level. When Zodie met with the staff that first day, she made it clear that she did not care what the union contract said; everyone at Sherrard is accountable. She proceeded to place transfer slips on the table stating that if anyone didn't like it, they should fill out a slip now. I always said that I wanted to buy a t-shirt that said "I survived the purge of 1974."

My most rewarding compliment came from the self-same Zodie Johnson who later became the Acting Superintendent of Detroit Public Schools. She wrote:

Dear Mr. Daniels,

Please accept my thanks for chairing the I.G.E. workshop at Sherrard Middle School. Your pleasantness and positive attitude in this position and in other activities at Sherrard added to the improvement of the entire school.

You are the kind of person who works well with children because you care. I hope in the future I shall have the opportunity to see you advance in the Detroit Public Schools.

You are the kind of person who likes people.

Sincerely,
Zodie A. Johnson

This letter arrived in December of 1975. It shows that with communication, hard work, and a caring attitude towards others, things can change. It took six years for feelings toward me, "the we don't need none" English teacher to change. I hope that this book by Cookie and Tom will also begin to change attitudes.

FINAL COMMENT

Both races need to stop labeling. What good does it do? Stereotyping just supports ignorance. It reminds ya of the story of the teenager who thought his parents were the dumbest people on the planet. Then at age 30, that same young man couldn't believe how smart his parents had become over the last 14 years.

We believe that education doesn't give you all the answers. Education helps you realize you do not know very much at all, and you need to continue to strive to learn as much as you can in order to actually have a worthy opinion. We all know the meatheads who seem to have all the answers. These are the people who make pronouncements in an authoritative way yet really don't know shit.

You can't even discuss with these people because of their narrow-mindedness.

We hope and pray that this book will open the readers' eyes and hearts to be able to better appreciate the other race. Cookie and Tom certainly have begun to do this with the help of Spider and Derek. God bless all of you.